The Consolation of Poetry

David Spurr

The Consolation of Poetry

Ten Lessons on Life and Death

PETER LANG

Bern · Berlin · Bruxelles · New York · Oxford

Bibliographic Information published by the Deutsche Nationalbibliothek
The Deutsche Nationalbibliothek lists this publication in the Deutsche Nationalbibliografie; detailed bibliographic data is available in the internet at http://dnb.d-nb.de.

Library of Congress Cataloging-in-Publication Data
A CIP catalog record for this book has been applied for
at the Library of Congress

"This Is Just to Say" By William Carlos Williams, from The Collected Poems, Vol. 1, 1909-1939, copyright ©1938 by New Directions Publishing Corp. Reprinted by permission of New Directions Publishing Corp.

Cover illustration: Vilhelm Hammershøi, Sunbeams (1900), Oil on canvas, 70 x 59, Ordrupgaard, Copenhagen. Foto: Anders Sune Berg.

ISBN 978-3-0343-4211-7 (Print)
E-ISBN 978-3-0343-4347-3 (E-PDF)
E-ISBN 978-3-0343-4348-0 (EPUB)
DOI 10.3726/b18477

© Peter Lang Group AG, International Academic Publishers, Bern 2021
www.peterlang.com

All rights reserved.
This publication has been peer reviewed.

All parts of this publication are protected by copyright. Any utilisation outside the strict limits of the copyright law, without the permission of the publisher, is forbidden and liable to prosecution. This applies in particular to reproductions, translations, microfilming, and storage and processing in electronic retrieval systems.

www.peterlang.com

Contents

Acknowledgments 9
Introduction 11

I   Seizing the Day 15

II   Loving Your Neighbor 27

III Forgiveness 39

IV   Finding the Center 53

V   Humility 65

VI   Discovery 77

VII Parting 91

VIII Dejection 103

IX   Self-Reliance 117

X   Taking Leave 129

But what does it mean to live esthetically, and what does it mean to live ethically? What is the esthetic in a person, and what is the ethical? To that I would respond: the esthetic in a person is that by which he spontaneously and immediately is what he is; the ethical is that by which he becomes what he becomes.

Kierkegaard

Acknowledgments

"This Is Just to Say" by William Carlos Williams, from *The Collected Poems, Vol. 1, 1909–1939*, copyright ©1938 by New Directions Publishing Corp. Reprinted by permission of New Directions Publishing Corp.
The Consolation of Poetry

Introduction

What are poets for? Every age since that of antiquity has had a different answer to this question. For our own age no one has had a better answer than the American poet Wallace Stevens. Stevens worked for most of his life as an executive at an insurance company in Hartford, Connecticut. Contrary to what one might expect, this prosaic occupation may have made him especially qualified to consider the potential importance of poetry to daily life. Insurance companies deal with risk, loss, and disaster. Those who make claims on them are often in a state of crisis from which they seek relief, if only in the form of monetary compensation. The analogy may seem farfetched, but Stevens saw poetry as a sort of insurance policy, a compensation for the kind of suffering caused not by fire or flood, but by the mere effort to live from day to day in the modern world. We are, he says, "an unhappy people in a happy world." Apart from us human beings, the world is happy, or at least not unhappy—so it seems when the northern lights blaze in the evening sky. But with our doubts, our loneliness and mortality, how can we hope to participate in such glory? Elsewhere, Stevens says that what gives birth to the poem is the fact that "we live in a place That is not our own and, much more, not ourselves, And hard it is in spite of blazoned days." Here it is not just the world of nature, but the world we have made that is somehow not our own, not ourselves: Stevens expresses the feeling, shared by other modern poets, of not being at home in the world. This homelessness, however, is that from which the poem springs; the poem's beauty, in the way its meaning derives from our condition of homelessness, offers a kind of consolation. In yet another poem, Stevens says that the function of the poet is to "reconcile us to ourselves" in the language of poetry: in "dark, pacific words" and their harmonies of sound and sense. It is not just that we do not feel at home in the world; Stevens suggests that we do not even feel at home with ourselves, and in this alienation, we need some sort of reconciliation with ourselves. This, then, is what the poet promises: nothing less than a sense of harmony with ourselves and our world. To say "ourselves and our world" implies that what the poem seeks to convey is not just about the self; it is about our relation to things outside us, to all that we are not: to the objects of the world and above all to other persons. The poem helps us to an awareness of others and to the fact that they are indeed other than we are. But the poem doesn't leave it at that, because poetry is the language of relation: it takes us out of ourselves in order to make contact with what we are not: it is William Wordsworth meeting the leech-gatherer, Walt Whitman taking in the runaway slave, Emily Dickinson imagining the condemned man. But the other—that thing which we are not—can also be a place, a thing, a common object, a memory. For Stevens it can be two pears on a green cloth; for W.B. Yeats, the memory of an island in a lake. The poem is a bridge to and a bond with the other, including the other within oneself; it is the way to life's enlargement. It is a consolation for our mortality.

Why then is poetry, especially modern poetry, sometimes difficult? Partly for this reason, that it takes us out of ourselves, away from the familiar phrases to which we are used to reducing our experience. It also seems difficult because it is a fresh way of saying, it makes something unique out of language, something unsaid before, and therefore it can seem obscure. But there is a mystery to beauty, even in language. As E.B. White has said, "A poet utterly clear is a trifle glaring." Poetry bears the same relation to everyday language as dance does to mere walking. Just as dance is a different movement of the body from that of walking, poetry is a different movement in language from talk about the weather. The difference between dancing and walking we see immediately and instinctively. The problem with poetry is that it is made of language, which signifies. Words have the specific function of referring to things or events, and therefore we might expect a poem to signify in the way that the weather report does. But of course the poem doesn't have that immediately practical meaning: poetry uses language as its material, gives it the music of rhythm and sound, and places it in a new context. To "understand" poetry is to hear this music and to entertain this context, even if they are unfamiliar. When Dickinson says, "I dwell in possibility—A fairer house than prose," she means that the poet creates not by using the familiar formulas of language but rather by exploring its hitherto unspoken possibilities.

The pages that follow draw on a wide variety of poems which can be read as offering guidance in what everyone faces every day: the question of how to live, of how to be. Each chapter brings together a series of poems in relation to a subject or a quality common to every life, such as dejection or forgiveness, in order to show the poet's insight into the nature of that quality. In each case we find that no two poets have the same experience of that feeling, that each defines it slightly differently, and so has something different to say about it. The result is that, while we may not get at the essence of the experience, we nonetheless see it from many sides, and we gain a sense of how that experience is lived by those who know how to speak of it most aptly. This is not to suggest that poets are models of virtue in their personal lives. The biographical evidence often proves quite the opposite. But what they have to offer is imagination and testimony. The imagination of what is possible, and the testimony to life that we find in poems, help us to think about what is most important to us, and offer examples of how others have faced the obstacles life puts before us. Wordsworth says to S.T. Coleridge at the conclusion of *The Prelude*, "What we have loved, Others will love, and we will teach them how."

Among the sorrows of the present age are those of nervousness, distraction, speed without destination, information without meaning, and noise in every sense of the word. But poetry promises relief from these things—not as mere escape, but as a way of restoring balance to our experience in an imperfect world. I do not claim, with Percy Shelley, that poets are the unacknowledged legislators of the world. But poets can be read as witnesses, and as counsellors in some of the things that matter most in life, for they have felt intensely and reflected deeply on what they have to say, and on how to say it in the way that most truly captures that feeling. We can learn from them in judging our own feelings and our relations with others. We can also derive solace from them. Dickinson writes, "If I can stop one heart from breaking—I shall not live in vain."

This book is for the common reader, unencumbered by literary prejudices and academic fashions. This is the reader whose imagination every poet must touch in order to be remembered; the reader who shall ultimately decide what great poetry is. For some readers, my presentations of the poems will serve as an introduction to some of the greatest poems in English. To others they offer an alternative approach to those poems through an ethical framework. Although many of the poems are quite famous, I don't assume the reader's prior knowledge of them. This is one of several ways in which I choose to depart from academic orthodoxy. The poems are read not primarily as aesthetic objects or as textual systems but as the work of real people who have something to say to us about life as they know it. For this reason, I often take the risk of identifying the poem's first-person speaker with the poet, and I consider the poet's real circumstances and surroundings at the time of the poem's composition. Every poem is an occasion, and whatever we can learn about the circumstances of that occasion may help us to understand why it was written and what it says. Another departure from orthodoxy is to seek to learn lessons from the poems. The poets of the seventeenth and eighteenth centuries took seriously the claim of the Roman poet Horace that the purpose of poetry was to "delight and instruct." More recent generations of critics have forgotten the second part of this double vocation. This book is an attempt to show how poetry might still instruct us and even console us in hard times. Even so, these cannot be lessons of the kind we learn in school, and as Whitman cautions, they cannot be learned completely. He says of his work, rather, that "it lets down the bars to a good lesson, And that to another, and every one to another still." In other words, the poem may not convey complete understanding, but it opens up the possibility of understanding. At its best, the power of imagination that poetry puts into words allows us to see what we might be. This power, combined with poetry's grounding in the reality of experience, makes it a source of meaning and value in the modern world.

In discussing these poems, I make frequent reference to the King James Version of the Bible, for two main reasons. The first is that the language of this translation—its vocabulary, cadences, metaphors, and images—is fundamental to English poetry from the seventeenth century to the present. The second is that more than any other historical source, the Bible addresses the same ethical questions addressed in English poetry, and therefore provides a starting point on how poetry treats those questions. Whatever misuse has been made of the Bible, it remains even for modern Western society the single most important source of ethical value for what it says about how to live and what makes life worth living. My use of the Bible, however, does not prevent me from citing other sources of insight into the nature of human conduct such as classical mythology, or modern thinkers such as Ralph Waldo Emerson and Sigmund Freud.

As many of the poems discussed in the following pages are too long to be quoted in full, I have selected the passages from them that are most relevant to my purpose. Conscious of the fact that the full impact of a poem can be conveyed only in its original form, I have confined myself to poems written in English. The emphasis of this book is on how to read a poem and on what to come away with from it. As to when and where to read, my experience is that the nuances of a poem are best received when the reader is fortunate enough to be able to read it aloud, in solitude, in quiet surroundings. But it is also possible to create a private space for yourself in a crowd. Either way, poetry offers not just consolation, but also a way of living in the modern world.

Seizing the Day

The ancient Greeks had two words for time: *kronos*, the time that passes, and *kairos*, the time of opportunity, the moment to be seized. The latter notion applies to every domain from medicine to the stock market to love. In Greek mythology *kairos* was represented as a god with a single lock of hair which had to be seized when he passed. If you missed, it was too late; the back of his head was bald. In the New Testament, *kairos* refers to the moment of fulfilment, when God intervenes in human destiny, as in Mark 1:15: "The time [*kairos*] is fulfilled, and the kingdom of God is at hand." The notion of *kairos* reminds us that life is fleeting, and that the rare chances for joy and goodness it offers must not escape us. The difficulty in life, as Hamlet discovered, is to distinguish between seizing the right moment and making a rash decision; the hesitation caused by this quandary makes for many missed opportunities, if also a few wise deferrals. Poets by nature, however, are not cautious, and they have made the need to seize the day one of the oldest themes in poetry. In the examples that follow, two poets of the Renaissance urge their ladies to seize the chance to love before it is too late. In later poets what is to be seized is more generally a passing moment of intensity, often made palpable in an image of natural beauty: field flowers, cherry blossoms, birdsong after rain. In each case the poem itself is a means of seizing the day, of capturing it in words. And in each case the real subject is time, and how little of it we have. In this sense, to seize the day is to live life itself with awareness and gratitude for what we are given.

This sense of life's intensity obtains even where an appeal to cast caution to the wind is used for a morally ambiguous purpose, as in Andrew Marvell's address "To his Coy Mistress." This is a dramatic poem from the seventeenth century, where the poet adopts the role of a libertine urging a lady to yield to his advances in the brief moment of life when his lust and her beauty are still intact. Here are the first few lines:

> Had we but world enough and time,
> This coyness, lady, were no crime.
> We would sit down, and think which way
> To walk, and pass our long love's day.

The poet's argument is skillful. He begins by granting that the lady would be justified in refusing him, if only they had all the time in the world; that is, if time moved so slowly that their day were to last as long as all of human history. In such a world, he could devote a hundred years to praising her eyes, two hundred to adoring each breast, and thirty thousand for all the rest. But instead, he hears "Time's winged chariot hurrying near": the time is short, and it will not be long before they both lie in the grave:

> The grave's a fine and private place,
> But none, I think, do there embrace.

That "I think" is a stroke of ironic brilliance. We do not know whether the poet's suit was successful, and there is some poignancy in the fact that the poem was published for the first time in 1681, three years after the poet himself was put in the grave. But while he is still very much alive, he concludes this poem with the urgent appeal to "let us sport us while we may"—to steal a length on time,

> And tear our pleasures with rough strife
> Through the iron gates of life:
> Thus, though we cannot make our sun
> Stand still, yet we will make him run.

The idea of tearing our pleasures is erotically charged, and one is tempted to dismiss Marvell's poem as a highly skillful treatment of a libertine mode of persuasion. The speaker's motives are hardly pure if the satisfaction of his lust requires the sacrifice of the lady's honor. But his argument is precisely that her honor will "turn to dust" with time, whereas the poet can see that in the present moment his mistress's "willing soul transpires At every pore with instant fires"—her desire burns as hotly as his, and her "coyness" is mere coquetry. Let us be generous, and grant that behind his cavalier rhetoric the poet has a nobler purpose than mere seduction. His greater subject is love, and he reminds us of the need to give and take love on those brief occasions in life when it is offered. Time does not favor those who wait passively for love, and for the joy it affords. The "iron gates of life" are there to be stormed. We must devour time before it devours us.

Marvell's contemporary Edmund Waller has a sweeter take on the subject of time passing, and on the urgency it imposes on youth and beauty. This is his "Song":

> Go, lovely Rose—
> Tell her that wastes her time and me,
> That now she knows,
> When I resemble her to thee,
> How sweet and fair she seems to be.
>
> Tell her that's young,
> And shuns to have her graces spied,
> That hadst thou sprung
> In deserts where no men abide,
> Thou must have uncommended died.
>
> Small is the worth
> Of beauty from the light retired:
> Bid her come forth,
> Suffer herself to be desired,
> And not blush so to be admired.

> Then die—that she
> The common fate of all things rare
> May read in thee;
> How small a part of time they share
> That are so wondrous sweet and fair!

This poem was famous in its time. It was written when the poet was in his twenties, and set to music by the composer Henry Lawes in 1635. It circulated widely as a song for more than 20 years before being published in Waller's collected poems of 1645. Waller presses his suit in a courtlier manner than Marvell: rather than "sporting" with his lady, he merely wishes her to show herself so that her beauty might be admired, and she "desired." Waller also relies less than Marvell does on abstract concepts of time; instead, the value of seizing the day is to be learned merely by looking upon a rose as it fades. Waller's poem is not, however, without its own ingenious conceits. It is the lady's concealment that causes the poet to send the rose as a messenger to the lady, so that he is obliged to address the rose instead of her. In its loveliness the rose is a fitting go-between. The instructions it receives from the poet are in four parts, each corresponding to a verse of the song. In the first, the rose is directed to go to the lady and tell her that the poet "resembles" or compares her to the rose in her sweetness and fairness, so that "now she knows" how she appears. It is as if she did not know her own beauty, and needed the sight of the rose in order to be conscious of it. For her to be unaware of her own beauty only increases her loveliness. But not to show it is to waste both her time and her lover, in the sense that he wastes away in longing.

The comparison between the rose and the lady is pursued in the second verse: just as a rose that blooms in the desert will die "uncommended," the same fate awaits the lady if she persists in hiding her beauty. The rose must therefore "bid her come forth" in the third verse, and it must "die" in the last. By witnessing the dying of the rose, the lady will learn the fate of all things "sweet and fair"—the very qualities praised in her, in the first verse.

Waller's song is written in the same mode as one written more than a century earlier by Pierre Ronsard to a lady named Cassandre. Ronsard's "Mignonne, allons voir si la rose" (Pretty maid, let us see if the rose) makes a similar comparison between the rose and the lady, as the poet urges her to go and see if the rose that bloomed in the morning has by evening lost its color. It has done so, of course, so that its example serves as a lesson to the lady: she must gather the blossoms of her youth before time does to her what it has done to the flower. Waller reworks this theme in an original and fanciful way that chides the lady for concealing herself. Rather than have the lady go to see the rose, the rose is sent to her as the poet's emissary—an emissary who communicates its message by means of its own death. Waller's rhetoric is less importunate and more lyrical than Marvell's, but both poets raise the specter of death as a reminder that what is not seized now from life will be gone tomorrow. Like Marvell, both Ronsard and Waller are advocates in the service of love; they argue the urgency of embracing its joys while there is still time.

We do not know the identity of the person addressed in Waller's poem, but it may be the lady Dorothea Sidney, eldest daughter of the Earl of Leicester. Waller himself was a gentleman and member of Parliament, but a lady of such high birth proved to be beyond his powers of persuasion. Samuel Johnson writes that "she was not to be subdued by the powers of verse, but rejected his addresses, it is said, with disdain." Instead, she married the Earl of Sunderland. Many years later she met Waller by chance, and asked him when he would again write such verses to her. His reply: "When you are as young, Madam, and as handsome as you were then." Kairos with his lock of hair had long since passed. If neither Waller's love nor the lady's beauty has lasted, the poem has. In 1920, the American poet Ezra Pound adapted the rhythms and images of Waller's song for the *Envoi* or final section of his poem "Hugh Selwyn Mauberley." But instead of sending the rose to his lady, Pound sends his book in its place. Unlike the rose, the book will preserve her graces "as roses might, in magic amber laid," and it "might, in new ages, gain her worshippers When our two dusts with Waller's shall be laid." Pound's poem is about "braving time" through art, which alone among human endeavors can outlive time. But the sense of Pound's poem is that art can preserve the beauty of fleeting moments only by sacrificing life itself, by laying the roses in magic amber. Eternal in art, beauty is fleeting in life.

Emily Dickinson evokes something like this idea in the wholly unexpected way that characterizes her verse. Rather than addressing another person, she speaks to the present moment directly, in an intimate and familiar manner:

> Oh Sumptuous moment
> Slower go
> That I may gloat on thee—
> 'Twill never be the same to starve
> Now I abundance see—
>
> Which was to famish, then or now—
> The difference of Day
> Ask him unto the Gallows led—
> With morning in the sky—

Dickinson lived most of her life in her father's ample brick house in the town center of Amherst, Massachusetts, in the mid-nineteenth century. As she moved about her household rounds, she wrote her brief poems on slips of paper she kept in a pocket of her white dress. The circumstances of her life were simple enough to allow her to see the beauty of the commonest moment. Her poem is more purely lyrical than those of Marvell and Waller, a more direct expression of the poet's powerful and intimate feeling. Though every poem is inspired by an occasion, Dickinson gives us little to go on regarding the precise nature of the moment that she so wants to last. In this she is true to her style: the particulars of an occasion are always secondary to the feeling it evokes. In this poem, one can nonetheless imagine her surprised by something as simple as the beauty of a summer morning in all its abundance. Or perhaps the sense of abundance does not derive from the external scene; it could be rather a sudden feeling within of the abundance of life itself, lived with sensuous intensity. The sensual quality is there at the poem's opening, where the initial "Oh" is repeated in a rapture of *o*'s throughout the first three lines. The last of these is in the word "gloat," where the poet appears to acknowledge the shamelessness of her pleasure, her total abandonment to it. The moment is addressed in the familiar "thee," as if to a lover whose departure she wishes to forestall. The stanza ends, however, on a reflective note. The poet realizes that the moment of abundance will make its absence all the more difficult to withstand in the future. Such an absence will be "to starve," and "famine," which to the present moment is as night to day.

The poem's concluding lines offer a vivid image for what has up to this point been fairly abstract language. On seeing the new day break, no feeling could be more intense than that of the man led to the gallows "with morning in the sky." The abundant "Day" of the previous line is not for him. He is banished from the feast. Dickinson appeals to the testimony of such a man, asking the reader to share his desperate point of view: the beauty of the newborn day is heightened in the extreme by the need to leave it behind so soon. In the condemned man's wish for the fateful dawn to come slowly, the poet conveys the strength of her own desire for her own moment to "Slower go." Dickinson was an eccentric woman, and visitors to the house on Main Street could be exhausted by the intensity of her personality. But in the poem she puts this ardor to the best possible use. The poem urges us to our own intensity of feeling, which is to be found at any moment, long before our last day. The thought of that day, however, must make our awareness of the present more acute. Dickinson says, in effect, seize the moment as if it were never to come again, for it will not.

Dickinson's poem marks a change from Marvell and Waller in her judgment of what is worth seizing. Her century marks the beginning of a sentiment where more than a moment of love is at stake. Instead, poets speak of their desire to hold fast to life itself. The promise of an afterlife, once held out by Christian doctrine, no longer was assured. If we live only once, then what shall we make of it? The poets of the late nineteenth century give thanks for life, whether in youthful blossom or decline. The late Victorian poet A.E. Housman locates the moment to seize in a particular time and place: Easter time in the speaker's twentieth year in the gently rolling hills of Shropshire, in the west of England.

> Loveliest of trees, the cherry now
> Is hung with bloom along the bough,
> And stands about the woodland ride
> Wearing white for Eastertide.
>
> Now, of my threescore years and ten,
> Twenty will not come again,
> And take from seventy springs a score,
> It only leaves me fifty more.
>
> And since to look at things in bloom
> Fifty springs are little room,
> About the woodlands I will go
> To see the cherry hung with snow.

This much-anthologized poem is originally from the collection known as *A Shropshire Lad* (1896), a book largely devoted to celebrating the young men from the country who answer the call to fight in the wars Britain waged to preserve its empire. Housman himself never went to war. Instead, he pursued a career as professor of Latin at London, and later at Cambridge. His life is the subject of Tom Stoppard's play "The Invention of Love" (1997), where the character of Frank Harris, also a writer, has little appreciation for *A Shropshire Lad*: "No one gets off; if you're not shot, hanged or stabbed, you kill yourself. Life's a curse, love's a blight, God's a blaggard, cherry blossom is quite nice." This last allusion is to "Loveliest of trees," which has nothing of the martial or patriotic, but when read in context it can be understood as expressing the speaker's sense of urgency to "look at things in bloom" before going off to a war from which he may not return.

In contrast to the private rapture of Dickinson's poem, this one has a classical restraint in keeping with Housman's studies in Latin literature. Each of the three stanzas of the poem, composed in simple rhyming couplets, takes a different approach to its subject. The first puts the speaker in a gentle natural landscape, where riding through the woods he sees the cherry trees in white blossom, as if dressed for the Easter season. The language is full of superlatives: the cherry is the loveliest of trees, wearing its finest white for the holiest time of year in the Christian calendar, when Christ's resurrection is celebrated as all of nature bursts forth in blossom.

From his contemplation of this natural scene, the poet turns in the second stanza to a mathematical calculation. The "now" of the poem's first line, which evoked delight in the present moment as an almost unexpected gift, here gives way to the "now" of the poet's life in terms the number of years he has left on earth for the enjoyment of such scenes. He has in mind Psalm 90 of the Bible: "The days of our years are threescore years and ten; and if by reason of strength they be fourscore years, yet is their strength labour and sorrow; for it is soon cut off, and we fly away."

With perhaps fifty years left of life, the youth still sees his time as short, as what remains of his allotted time. This is the thought expressed in the final stanza, which ends with a resolution to "look at things in bloom" while there is still time left. But at the end, both the image and the season have shifted: this time it is "the cherry hung with snow" rather than the tree's white blossom, meaning that we have moved from Eastertide to autumn, when an early snow covers the still unharvested fruit. Housman has set up a running allegory between the cultivation cycle of the cherry and the life span of the poet, so that the poet imagines his remaining years as leading from the bloom of youth to the winter of old age. The cherry hung with snow, however, is a very different vision from that of the cherry blossom in spring. The repetition of "hung" might give us pause. If at Eastertide the bough hung with blossom appears as a mere ornament of the season, the cherry hung with snow is a more striking and incongruous image, that of an early frost which kills the fruit. It is the equivalent in nature of the fate of Dickinson's condemned man led to the gallows, so that the final line of Housman's poem casts a chill over a poem which otherwise seems to claim little more than the delights of a ramble through the countryside. In this way, Housman suggests that he will derive joy from change and life's decline as much as from its youthful beauty. The moment he wants to seize is therefore nothing less than the rest of his life—a life he sees as lasting, in human terms, no longer than the brief season of the cherry. The challenge he sets for himself, and the resolution he makes in the poem's simple understatement, is to behold the beauty of that life fully, both in youth and in old age.

It takes nothing from the beauty of Housman's poem to know that when he wrote it he was 36, not 20, and that he was living in the north of London, not the pastoral land of Shropshire. Shropshire is a county of great natural beauty, where the River Severn meanders through green hills and ancient English villages. But it is likely that when Housman wrote these poems he had never even been to Shropshire, though he had grown up in neighboring Worcestershire. However, Shropshire was real enough in his imagination. In the 40th poem of *A Shropshire Lad* he evokes that country as "the land of lost content [...] The happy highways where I went And cannot come again." We might take this as a confession that the resolution of "Loveliest of trees" has not been kept. In the later verses the poet has given in to the sense of loss, thereby confirming the bleak interpretation of Housman that Frank Harris volunteers in Stoppard's play. But if the happy season of 20 years will not return, its youthful resolve is nonetheless what continues to inspire Housman, both as a man and as a poet, and that is also inspiration for the reader.

Robert Frost's "The Last Mowing" is also set in a particular time and place, a New Hampshire farm in the 1920s, and in this case the setting is not imaginary but authentic to the poet's life. The poem is from Frost's collection *West-Running Brook* of 1928:

> There's a place called Far-away Meadow
> We never shall mow in again,
> Or such is the talk at the farmhouse:
> The meadow is finished with men.
> Then now is the chance for the flowers
> That can't stand mowers and plowers.
> It must be now, though, in season
> Before the not mowing brings trees on,
> Before trees, seeing the opening,
> March into a shadowy claim.
> The trees are all I'm afraid of,
> That flowers can't bloom in the shade of;
> It's no more men I'm afraid of;
> The meadow is done with the tame.
> The place for the moment is ours
> For you, oh tumultuous flowers,
> To go to waste and go wild in,
> All shapes and colors of flowers,
> I needn't call you by name.

Frost is a poet who makes a kind of dramatic character out of himself. In this case, he figures as a kind of misplaced romantic in the practical world of the farm. He leaves the talk of the farmhouse to seek his own moment of meaning in a transitory natural scene. The poem divides its subject into three parts, beginning with the naming of Far-away Meadow and its condition of obsolescence: it will no longer be mowed, perhaps because its distance from the farmhouse makes the mowing more trouble than it's worth, perhaps because the farm itself is in decline. This is a poem of last things: the last mowing has been done, this is the last season in which there will be flowers, and it is the last chance for the poet to see them. The finality of the occasion lends it urgency.

Apart from last things, Frost is consistently drawn to out-of-the-way, lonely places, and this is no exception. He sees a rare chance in the fact that the meadow is now "finished with men," that is, with farmers who think of land only in terms of its return on their labor. The far meadow is now the place of a propitious moment in time: "now is the chance for flowers" that would otherwise be cut down by the mowers. But the life of the flowers is limited to a single season, because once the trees begin to grow on the fallow field, their shade will put an end to the flowers' bloom. The trees are given the character of an army, seeing the opening left by the absent mowers, and marching in to make their own claim on the meadow.

The final lines of the poem turn to the poet's feeling of solidarity with the flowers. His fears for them no longer have to do with the mowers, but with the invasion of the meadow by the natural, untamed force of invasive trees. He also appears to have changed places. From the farmhouse and its talk, he has gone out to the meadow itself, at least in imagination. This move is signaled by a surprising shift in the use of his pronouns. In the second line of the poem, the first-person "we" put the poet in the company of the mowers. But now the first-person is used to put him in the company of the flowers: "The place for the moment is ours." Like Dickinson in her address to the "sumptuous moment," Frost speaks to the flowers as his intimates. He has shifted allegiances, from the ordered and domestic world of farm work to the flowers' untamed wildness. He encourages their tumultuous profusion and variety in "all shapes and colors."

Poets sometimes speak directly to objects in nature, or to time. Waller gives instruction to the rose; Dickinson entreats the "moment" to tarry, as if it were a lover about to leave. When Frost tells the flowers that he needn't call them by name, he is saying something fundamental about language as the act of naming. Naming things is a form of human mastery over nature. In the Book of Genesis (I.2), Adam is given dominion over the earth, which includes the power to name every living creature, for naming things is itself a form of mastery over them. In this poem, Frost recognizes that for the flowers of the field, "done with men," it no longer makes sense to call them by the names given them by men. Their wild freedom puts them beyond human nomenclature. Beyond this, the poem sets up an opposition between "need" and "waste." Far-away Meadow has become a place of waste in the economy of the farm, because its grass is no longer needed for mowing. Likewise, at the end of the poem, the absence of the need to name the flowers derives from the fact that they "go to waste" in their wildness. The paradox is that for the flowers this moment of "waste" is their only chance at life, and the poet's only chance to witness the beauty of the meadow in bloom. But to see it he will have to "waste his time," to abandon his duties at the farm for a time in order to seek out the distant field. The fellowship between the poet and the flowers, then, lies in their common thriving on what the world judges as wasteful. Just as the brief moment after the last mowing and before the onset of the trees is seized by the flowers in order to bloom, so that same moment is seized by the poet as the source of his inspiration.

This is one of many poems in which Frost celebrates wasteful activities: swinging birches, stopping by woods on a snowy evening, mending walls that keep nothing in or out. For nine years Frost worked a farm in Derry, New Hampshire. But he was never successful at it, and eventually had to give it up. This poem might help to explain why. Paradoxically, it was the more "wasteful" activity of writing poems that eventually sustained him, and even in this poem, he reaps a harvest from a meadow gone to waste. The economy of poetry is different from that of household duties and farm chores. We can imagine Dickinson neglecting her household duties as she entreats the sumptuous moment to stay with her, just as Frost would leave aside his farming chores to see the far-off meadow in bloom. But in each case, the poem itself proves a return on the investment in something beyond naming.

The recent past has brought us a more enigmatic way of capturing life as it passes. Such is W.S. Merwin's "For the Anniversary of My Death." This poem of thirteen short lines, written without punctuation, contemplates the day, still unknown, when the poet will die. The point is that just as we celebrate the day of our birth, we can also contemplate the day of our death with a serenity that, paradoxically, allows us to seize the joy of the present moment. In other words, like his birthday, the poet also lives every year the day of his death, not knowing which day that is: "Every year without knowing it I have passed the day." His poem is written for that day, as a kind of advance commemoration. What the poet seizes first is the idea of the fatal anniversary, which, for all he knows, is this very day. His first image is that of "last fires" of life, which will wave in bidding him adieu. In another image, his metaphor for the day of his death is the traditional one of the voyage: not his own, but that of the "silence" that has set out on a long journey to reach him, like the beam of a star which has gone out, but whose light continues on its way toward us on earth. Merwin here relies on the modern knowledge that the light of stars in the firmament reaches us long after those stars are extinguished. In like manner, since Merwin's death in 2019, we might think of the poem in this way, as the light of imagination that still shines after the poet has expired.

The second part of this poem moves from this vision to a more concrete evocation of the present time and place—a life lived among men and women and the things of nature. Life itself is a "strange garment" in which the poet finds himself clothed. The garment is his present condition, where he is surprised at the earth, at the love of a woman, and at "the shamelessness of men." The comparison of this life to a strange garment would seem to suggest that death would be a form of liberation, where the poet would no longer be subject to the accidents of time and place, and to the strangeness of his surroundings. But such a view fails to take into account the difference between the cosmic emptiness of the afterlife and the rich, if imperfect, texture of life in the present. "The shamelessness of men" is one of the conditions of the poem—it was published in 1967 at the height of the Vietnam War. But if this circumstance is a source of sorrow, the strange garment of life, by contrast, is embroidered with rich design. Its wearer is privileged with surprise, among them the song of the wren, singing after three days of rain.

The poem lacks punctuation, but it does have a certain shape on the page. The various objects of surprise are evoked in successively longer lines, yet all fall, both graphically and in their respective images, under the cover of the long line of life's strange garment. Of particular interest is the poet's surprise at the love of a woman, the word "love" being placed in the exact center of the block of type forming the poem's second section. To be surprised at that love and to feel it as part of the strangeness of life is to acknowledge it as an act of grace, an unexpected blessing for which the poet implicitly gives thanks. The poet is not necessarily looking for the moment to seize, but when it comes on him unawares, he knows enough to write it down. He does not so much seize the moment as he allows it to seize him. Merwin shares with Dickinson the purely lyrical expression of an intimate feeling, while he shares with the poets of Marvell's age the art of rendering personal experience by means of an ingenious conceit.

Merwin wrote the poem at a house in the South of France where he was staying in 1967. In 1984, he told an interviewer that most of the poems in *The Lice*, which includes this poem, were written in a state of dejection, when "I got to the point where I thought the future was so bleak that there was no point in writing anything at all. And so the poems kind of pushed their way upon me when I wasn't thinking of writing. I would be out growing vegetables and walking around the countryside when all of a sudden I'd find myself writing a poem, and I'd write it."[1]

Merwin's interest in Zen Buddhism is reflected in this poem. Unlike other poems we have seen, there is no calculation, no argument here. The absence of punctuation is a graphic counterpart to the flow of time in which the mortal anniversary passes without being marked. It corresponds as well to the poet's attitude of receptivity—a reluctance to intervene with stops and starts in the language given to him, and the wish to leave it as pure as it has come to him, directly from experience.

The poem ends with an image of the poet in a gesture of homage after the song of a wren marks the end of the three days of rain:

> Hearing the wren sing and the falling cease
> And bowing not knowing to what

The sense of peace and reverence evoked by this ending has an ancient source, which continues to resonate even today. It distantly recalls the forty days of rain that flooded the earth in the eighth chapter of Genesis, and the peace that reigned when at last "the rain from heaven was restrained" (Gen. 8: 2). Merwin's singing wren is a humbler cousin of the dove that announces the end of the flood, and where Noah built an altar giving thanks to God, the modern poet hardly knows to whom or what he bends his head. We should take this not as a sign of faithlessness, but rather as a sign of profound humility, like the awareness that every year without knowing it we live the anniversary of our death. That death will not alter the course of nature. The chapter of Genesis ends with the assurance that "the earth remaineth, seedtime and harvest, and cold and heat, and summer and winter, and day and night shall not cease." Merwin's reverence is to the simple things that life on earth offers here and now, to those who are ready to accept them. It is a way of seizing the day.

The poems we have reviewed here resort to a variety of devices in communicating a basic human truth. Marvell and Waller evoke the ephemeral nature of a young woman's beauty and of their own passions. Dickinson accepts the invitation to seize the moment, but wants to delay its passing. Housman makes a resolution to devote the rest of his life to the appreciation of life itself, so that all of life becomes his moment. Frost's more homely vision is occasioned by the circumstances of agricultural economy, but it ultimately revels in the wildness of a moment and place removed from human order. Of all these ways of capturing the moment, Merwin's is the most oblique, and its Zen-like receptivity stands in stark opposition to Marvell's resolve to tear through the iron gates of life. And yet Merwin's poem ends with the feeling of gratitude for life that is at least implied in every poem cited here.

In addition to this gratitude, what each of these poems has in common is the thought of death. Marvell reminds his mistress that when they lie in the grave, it will be too late to embrace. Waller commands the rose to die as an instruction against his lady's retirement. Dickinson's condemned man sees his last morning in the sky. Housman derives a sense of urgency from calculating the remaining years of his life. Frost must go to the far-away meadow before the flowers stop blooming forever. And Merwin's reverence for life is occasioned by the perceived imminence of death. As Marvell makes clear from the beginning, there would be no reason to seize the day if there were always a tomorrow to which it could be put off. There is not always a tomorrow, as each poet seems keenly aware, and it is precisely that awareness of potential absence, that sense of death's imminence, that intensifies the poet's experience of the here and now. Wallace Stevens has written that death is the mother of beauty. Knowing that life is mortal heightens our consciousness of its quality and our appreciation of its beauty. The same can be said of love: if we do not give and receive it now, then when?

Note

1 David L. Elliott, "An Interview with W.S. Merwin." *Contemporary Literature* 39 (Spring 1988), 1–25, p. 6.

Loving Your Neighbor

The ancient injunction to love your neighbor as yourself seems straightforward enough, at least in principle, until you try to say what it actually means. When God gives this command to Moses in Leviticus (19:18), he forbids his people from seeking revenge or from bearing a grudge. In doing so, he seems to order restraint rather than active love. But when Jesus, before the Pharisees in Matthew 22:39, cites the commandment, "Thou shalt love thy neighbour as thyself," he uses the same verb for "love"—*agape*—that he has just used for the first great commandment, "Thou shalt love the Lord thy God with all thy heart" (22:37). This makes love in the New Testament something active and willing rather than mere forbearance from vengeance. This difference between the Old and New Testaments has opened the way to a host of modern interpretations of the law that binds human beings to one another. The eighteenth-century philosopher Immanuel Kant recognizes our obligation to help the poor, but cautions against doing so in such a way as to humiliate the poor by making them feel they are objects of charity. Rather, we should act as if our help were merely what they deserve, or at most a "slight service of love," so as to allow them to maintain their self-respect.[1] In the twentieth century, C.S. Lewis points out that the way you love your neighbor as yourself depends on how you feel about yourself. There may be times when you hate yourself, but in the long run you still hope for your own welfare; "love is not an affectionate feeling, but a steady wish for the loved person's ultimate good as far as it can be obtained."[2] Finally, the philosopher Emmanuel Levinas tells us that our neighbor, who is after all someone other than we are, is ultimately unknowable to us. Yet we have an innate obligation to that other person *as* other, because our own humanity depends on the nature of our relation to others. Fundamentally, loving one's neighbor is an act of imagination: the ability to go beyond the sphere of the self and enter the world of the other.

What philosophers tell us in theory, poets show us in personal testimony and direct address. They give us actual human situations, with all the subtleties of feeling that belong to one person's relation to another: compassion for suffering, tolerance of idiosyncrasy, the longing for connection, the recognition of a common fate. The language of poets is more concrete than that of philosophy, more immediate, and ultimately more powerful. There is Walt Whitman, whose love for his fellow creatures on earth knew no bounds. *Leaves of Grass* is Whitman's hymn to the American people and their landscape. The collection is one of the first to have been written in free verse, with long lines that extend to embrace every living being within its panoramic scope. It was first published in 1855, when the movement to abolish slavery was at its height. Whitman's own attitude toward slavery had evolved over the years. It was crystallized in 1854 by an infamous enforcement of the Fugitive Slave Law, in which the federal government intervened to arrest a runaway slave who had escaped from Virginia to take refuge in Boston. The incident emboldened Whitman to publish poems expressing sympathy with the plight of his fellow Americans of African descent. When put together, different parts of his work tell the story of the fate of slaves: their sale at the auction block, the violent treatment they suffer, and for a few, the escape north to freedom.

For a period in 1848, Whitman worked as editor of a newspaper, the New Orleans *Crescent*. During this time, he would have had the opportunity to witness the slave auctions held in various parts of the city. One of the venues was the neoclassical Rotunda of the Merchants' Exchange. An 1842 engraving by William Henry Brooke shows slaves being sold at the center of the large room, as paintings and estate properties are also auctioned off on the periphery. The atmosphere is festive, with ladies in brightly colored gowns and children playing. A family of slaves stands, half-naked and impassive, on the auction block. Inspired by such scenes, a passage from Whitman's "I Sing the Body Electric" begins with the image of "a man's body at auction." The poet adopts the ironic conceit of assisting the auctioneer by addressing the crowd in praise of the man's body. "Gentlemen, look on this wonder":

> In this head the all-baffling brain,
> In it and below it the makings of heroes.
> Examine these limbs, red, black, or white, they are cunning in tendon and nerve,
> They shall be stript that you may see them.

Then, abandoning the irony, Whitman speaks of the man's heart not just as an organ but as the source of human feeling:

> There swells and jets a heart, there all passions, desires, reachings, aspirations,
> (Do you think they are not there because they are not express'd in parlors and lecture-rooms?)

Whitman is an epic poet, who does for America what Homer did for Greece and Virgil for Rome: he defines the destiny of his people in a manner that is visionary in its panoramic sweep and precise in the most intimate aspects of daily life. In the present passage he finds that destiny in a man reduced to the humblest possible state. He names the slave prophetically as the father of generations, of "populous states and rich republics," of "countless immortal lives with countless embodiments and enjoyments." The passage concludes with a question addressed to the crowd of bidders: How do they know who shall come from the man's offspring, and more provocatively, "Who might you find you have come from yourself, if you could trace back through the centuries?" The poem's language thus progresses from the man's body to his affective faculties, and from there to his role, like Abraham's, as the father of future generations. The final question makes the point that the body for sale is that of a man no less human than his bidders, with whom he might share the same blood. The poem recalls the inscription on the widely distributed medallion produced in 1787 by the abolitionist Josiah Wedgwood. The design of the medallion depicts a slave raising his chains in appeal, with the legend, "Am I not a man and a brother?"

This section of "I Sing the Body Electric" is followed by the scene of a woman's body at auction; she is likewise seen as the mother of future generations. Again the poet asks a series of questions:

> Have you ever loved the body of a woman?
> Have you ever loved the body of a man?
> Do you not see that these are exactly the same to all in all nations and times all over the earth?

If the human body is universal, then so is human nature. Whitman's rhetorical questions serve as an impassioned plea for equality and for human love in every sense of the word. A passage from the great poem that came to be known as *Song of Myself* puts the slave woman in the company of other inhabitants of the city:

> The quadroon girl is sold at the auction-stand, the drunkard nods by the bar-room stove,
> The machinist rolls up his sleeves, the policeman travels his beat, the gate-keeper marks who pass [...]

In slave-holding society, a quadroon was a person of one-quarter African descent. As the other three quarters were of European descent, such persons often passed for "white." The quadroon girl, a frequently eroticized figure in nineteenth-century art and literature, literally embodies the absence of natural difference between "races." The poem names her in a catalogue of persons of various conditions so as to mark their common humanity and the poet's identity with them on that basis.

Though Whitman declares his identity with every one of his fellow men and women, he does so especially with those who suffer at the hands of others. These include the runaway slave in *Song of Myself*:

> I am the hounded slave, I wince at the bite of the dogs,
> Hell and despair are upon me, crack and again crack the marksmen,
> I clutch the rails of the fence, my gore dribs, thinn'd with the ooze of my skin,
> I fall on the weeds and stones,
> The riders spur their unwilling horses, haul close,
> Taunt my dizzy ears and beat me violently over the head with whip-stocks.

The capture and punishment of the runaway slave are made into a modern scene of crucifixion, with the fence for cross, taunting pursuers for mocking soldiers, and the victim's despair. More than this, the poet speaks in the first person; he becomes the slave. He hears the sound of the guns, he feels the bite of the dogs, the wound and the blows of the whip-stocks. Whitman's lines put into action his solemn affirmation: "I am the man, I suffer'd, I was there." The words echo those spoken by Pontius Pilate in releasing Jesus of Nazareth to the hostile crowd in John 19:5: "Behold the man," except that where Pilate washed his hands of the affair, Whitman becomes one with the condemned man. Jesus wears the crown of thorns, and is about to be crucified. By implication, the suffering of the hounded slave is rendered Christlike; the poet becomes one with him in an act of profound identity.

In another section of the same poem, Whitman envisions the runaway slave who has escaped his confinement. This time he does more than evoke a scene; he tells a quite moving story:

> The runaway slave came to my house and stopt outside,
> I heard his motions crackling the twigs of the woodpile,
> Through the swung half-door of the kitchen I saw him limpsy and weak,
> And went where he sat on a log and led him in and assured him,
> And brought water and filled a tub for his sweated body and bruis'd feet,
> And gave him a room that enter'd from my own, and gave him some coarse clean clothes,
> And remember perfectly well his revolving eyes and his awkwardness,
> And remember putting plasters on the galls of his neck and ankles;
> He stayed with me a week before he was recuperated and pass'd north,
> I had him sit next to me at table, my fire-lock lean'd in the corner.

Whitman writes as if his house were one of the stops on the "underground railroad," the secret system of safe houses by which escaped slaves could be conveyed toward Canada and thus to freedom. One of the routes passed through Brooklyn, New York, where Whitman lived in the 1850s.

Whether Whitman's story in this poem is biographical or imagined, it has the texture of lived experience: the sound of the man outside the house, the sight of him through the kitchen door, the care given to his wounds, his place at the poet's table. There is reason to believe the poet when he says that he remembers it all perfectly well. Among the wealth of details packed into these lines, several stand out as more than mere description of the scene. First, the poet's gesture of washing the slave's feet recalls the passage in John (13:1–17) where Jesus washes the feet of his disciples just before the feast of the Passover, his last supper with them. Where Jesus has filled a basin to wash the dust from his disciples' feet, Whitman fills a tub for the bruised feet of the slave. The slave's revolving eyes and awkwardness recall the protests of the disciples, who do not understand this humble gesture on the part of their Lord and Master. But Jesus's explanation is clear: "If I then, your Lord and Master, have washed your feet, ye also ought to wash one another's feet" (13:14). His message, like Whitman's, is one of equality among his followers. It is also a powerful example of humility. Whitman's own attitude toward the slave is one not just of humility but of trust: the room assigned to his guest is entered from the poet's own room. The communication between the rooms suggests that, by inhabiting a common space, they share a common status as human beings. In his gestures of humility, Whitman is animated by the same spirit that moves Kant to caution against a condescending form of charity. Instead, he implies that our help is merely what the less fortunate deserve. The crowning image of Whitman's scene is that of the fire-lock leaned in the corner, beside the table shared by the two men. Whitman has left the gun within reach of the slave, in effect putting his own life in the hands of his guest, just as the slave's life has been put in his. His relation to the slave has passed from one of charitable care to one of equal footing with his guest, and supreme trust in the power of human love. It is as if Whitman wanted to say, with Christ, "I have given you an example, that you should do as I have done" (John 13:15).

For the two men to sit together at the table evokes one of the most ancient images of Western civilization: the mutual respect of guest and host. The Greeks called it *xenia*. In another part of *Song of Myself*, Whitman uses the same image to signify his inclusion of all fellow human beings, regardless of their status in the world:

> This is the meal equally set, this is the meat for natural hunger,
> It is for the wicked just the same as the righteous, I make appointments with all,
> I will not have a single person slighted or left away,
> The kept-woman, sponger, thief, are hereby invited,
> The heavy-lipped slave is invited, the venerealee is invited;
> There shall be no difference between them and the rest.

This is a list of social castoffs—the compromised, the criminal, the enslaved, the diseased. The meal of which they partake equally is that of human life, a condition in which there is no difference between them and the rest: all have a natural hunger, not just for food but for human love. The meal also serves as a figure for the poem, a song of the poet's self in its capacity to celebrate human life without distinction.

In another catalogue of fellow men and women, the poet names a new bride and the president alongside a drug addict and a prostitute:

> The opium-eater reclines with rigid head and just-open'd lips,
> The prostitute draggles her shawl, her bonnet bobs on her tipsy and pimpled neck,
> The crowd laugh at her blackguard oaths, the men jeer and wink to each other,
> (Miserable! I do not laugh at your oaths nor jeer you;)

The figure of the prostitute echoes that of the woman taken in adultery "in the very act," in John 8. In that story, the woman's accusers bring her before Jesus in order to provoke him. They cite the punishment for adultery ordered in Leviticus 20:10: that she shall be put to death. Jesus's initial response is to write on the ground, as if preoccupied by other matters, refusing to act as a judge. When the accusers persist, he challenges them by inviting the one who is without sin to cast the first stone. He then turns again to his writing.

One by one the men leave, until Jesus is left alone with the woman. He tells her, "Neither do I condemn thee: go, and sin no more" (8:11). The point is not that the woman is innocent, but that human beings are equal in the eyes of God. John does not tell us what Jesus has written, and this silence has occasioned a great deal of speculation among readers of the Bible. What seems important, in retrospect, is the act of writing itself. Perhaps Jesus is writing down the sins of the accusers. Or, more meaningfully, perhaps he is writing the higher law he has cited in Matthew 7:12: "Therefore all things whatsoever ye would that men should do to you, do ye even so to them: for this is the law and the prophets." In Whitman's story, the poet looks on as the prostitute suffers the cruelty of the men around her, and he, too, writes. His writing is both an act of witnessing and an expression of solidarity with the prostitute: "I do not laugh at your oaths nor jeer you." The poet's address to her separates him from the other men in its compassion. His sympathy for her extends to her clumsy movements and blemished skin, where she seems to wear the stain of her condition on her very body.

Whitman's compassion for the victims of slavery and prostitution is in keeping with his belief that the human body is sacred, whereas what slavery and prostitution have in common is the desecration of the body by making it a saleable object. *Leaves of Grass* contains the following lines written "To a common prostitute":

> Be composed – be at ease with me – I am Walt Whitman, liberal and lusty as Nature,
> Not till the sun excludes you do I exclude you,
> Not till the waters refuse to glisten for you and the leaves to rustle for you, do my words refuse to glisten and rustle for you.
>
> My girl I appoint with you an appointment, and I charge you that you make preparation to be worthy to meet me,
> And I charge you that you be patient and perfect till I come.
>
> Till then I salute you with a significant look, that you do not forget me.

The title of the poem recalls a line from *Song of Myself*: "What is commonest, cheapest, nearest, easiest, is Me." In Whitman's language, the "common" quality of the prostitute is transformed into something the poet embraces as himself. Here the poet takes a more active role than in the earlier scene. He includes the woman as an object of his goodwill by recognizing her, like his "liberal and lusty" self, as belonging to nature; he would no more exclude her from his blessing than he would exclude the sun, the waters, and the trees. By the same token, his words are part of nature as well: through the poetic elements of image and sound, they glisten and rustle on the leaves of his book just as the water does and the leaves of the trees.

The second verse, "My girl I appoint you," is Whitman's adaptation of Jesus's address to the woman taken in adultery. It is an exalted role for him to assume, but the concept of sin is not part of Whitman's language; he is not a Christian in any traditional sense except in the essential thing, that he loves his neighbor as himself. Rather than command the woman to sin no more and dismiss her, he engages her personally. Prostitutes are available by appointment, and Whitman plays on this convention by making another sort of appointment with her, one that involves preparation on her part. He charges her to "be patient and perfect till I come," reinforcing his message with a "significant look" so that she will remember him. Jesus has likewise said to his followers, "Therefore you also must be ready, for the Son of Man is coming at an hour you do not expect" (Matthew 24:44). In Whitman's case, the patience he counsels is in keeping with his earlier wish for the girl to be composed and at ease with him. If he desires her perfection, it is the kind of perfection to be found in the elements of nature, like the sun and the glistening waters, free of artifice and adulteration. Whitman can hardly compel the woman to change her trade, but he can attempt to relieve her fear, and to put his trust in her—to reassure her of her humanity.

Loving your neighbor can take other forms than compassion for human suffering. Robert Frost demonstrates another kind of neighborly relation in "Mending Wall." The poem has its origins in Frost's farming life, and in the kind of stone walls that mark the boundary lines between New England farms. The first few lines of the poem explain why the walls need yearly repair. In winter, the shift in frozen ground causes the stones to spill over. Hunters trying to get at their game also cause damage. For these reasons, the poet and his neighbor engage in a ritual every spring: they meet on a given day to replace the stones one by one, each man on his side of the wall. The problem for the poet is that the ritual has no practical value, since the wall separates only an apple orchard from a pine grove.

The poem takes a dramatic form in the exchange between the poet and his neighbor, though this turns out to be a dialogue of mutual misunderstanding. When the poet tells his neighbor that "My apple trees will never get across And eat the cones under his pines," the neighbor replies with an old adage: "Good fences make good neighbors." Mischievously, the poet presses his point:

> '*Why* do they make good neighbors? Isn't it
> Where there are cows? But here there are no cows.
> Before I built a wall I'd ask to know
> What I was walling in or walling out,
> And to whom I was like to give offence [...]'

The neighbor won't be questioned on the matter, and continues about his work:

> I see him there
> Bringing a stone grasped firmly by the top
> In each hand, like an old-stone savage armed.
> He moves in darkness as it seems to me,
> Not of woods only and the shade of trees.
> He will not go behind his father's saying,
> And he likes having thought of it so well
> He says again, 'Good fences make good neighbors.'

The neighbor's refusal to listen to reason recalls a poem by Wordsworth where he asks a little cottage girl how many children are in her family. "We are seven," she replies, counting a sister and brother who lie in their graves. The poet points out that if those two are gone, "then ye are only five." But the girl insists on having it her way, repeating, "Nay, we are seven." For her, the dead brother and sister still count.

Like Wordsworth, Frost writes in a conversational, anecdotal manner; he is the gentleman farmer telling an amusing story about a stubborn neighbor. The poem is sometimes read as a simple affirmation of the neighbor's saying, but in fact the poet questions the saying on rational grounds. The concluding lines mark a difference between the poet, who is likely to question things, and the neighbor, whose unquestioning way of life is inherited from generations of ritual and tradition. To the poet, the neighbor moves in the darkness of primitive superstition; the neighbor can only repeat his father's saying, and do things as they always have been done.

The poem relates to our theme insofar as, out of respect for his neighbor, the poet accepts the ritual, taking part in it every spring. His questions are posed playfully, as part of a task he calls "just another kind of outdoor game," even if his neighbor takes it more seriously. This difference in understanding is great enough for the final lines to expose a deep divide between the modern mind of practical reason and the more ancient mind of ancestral tradition. But the neighborly feeling manifested here is that of each man's tolerance of the other despite the evident difference in their respective views of the world. The poet has learned to live with the "darkness" of his neighbor's world, just as the neighbor tolerates the poet's questions as one would the questions of a child. We can conclude that if good fences don't necessarily make good neighbors, then what does make them is the mutual acceptance of the other. Neither man entirely understands the other, but their tolerance of difference is what preserves peace, and even good humor between neighbors.

The Scottish poet Iain Crichton Smith lived during his later years in a house on the River Nant in the Argyll Highlands. His poem entitled "Neighbour" is a variation on Frost's theme written as a kind of secular prayer. The poet wishes for a bridge to be built across a stream, where he sees a neighbor standing in his dungarees on a cool morning. The sight of his neighbor awakens in the poet a desire for connection and common ground with him. This desire makes the poet appeal to the things of nature. He calls for the flowers—snowdrops—to spread wherever they may, and for the blackbird to sing across the fences. Finally, the poet addresses the enigmatic neighbor:

> [...] if the rain falls on you,
> let it fall on me also
> from the same black cloud
> that does not recognise gates.

From *A Country for Old Men*, 2000

The poem expresses the wish for simple human relation in a natural landscape whose beauty renders trivial the human attempt at marking boundaries. The first part of the poem moves in a series of simple images from the imagined bridge to the neighbor's house, to the neighbor himself. The neighbor is dressed in clothing that avoids all pretentions to formality, and which perfectly suits the splendor of the fresh Highland morning. The sequence of images follows the imagined itinerary of the poet himself, were such a bridge ever to be built. Now the function of a bridge is to allow a river to be crossed, but by connecting the two banks of the river, it also defines them in a completely new relation to each other. On one hand, the bridge represents the human triumph of human will over the limits imposed by the natural landscape. On the other hand, it permits the narrative of "crossing," the story of the journey from one side to the other, where possibly the poet has never been, to the neighbor he may never have met. In this respect, the imagined bridge is an opening unto the unknown.

If the first part of the poem imagines a human triumph over nature by means of the bridge, the next two parts tell of nature's indifference to the human boundaries of fences and gates. Judging by the flowering of the snowdrops, the season is early spring. The poet addresses the white flowers and the blackbird again in the subjunctive mode of desire. In bidding them to spread where they will and to sing without regard to fenced boundaries, he affirms his own desire to do likewise, to roam the land freely and to sing his transcendent song. However, the stark black and white of the natural images—"snowdrops" and "blackbird"—hints at something other than the Romantic ideal of human harmony with nature, and suggests that Crichton Smith has a darker theme. The final stanza is ostensibly addressed to the neighbor seen in the distance, but again expresses the will of the poet—that the rain of the "black cloud" that hovers over both of them should fall on him as it falls on his neighbor. As the black cloud and the rain are traditional images of human suffering and death, Crichton Smith seems to invoke the mortality that he has in common with his neighbor. Ultimately, nature's indifference to human boundaries includes its indifference to human life, on which nature puts its own limit.

This then, is the most compelling reason for neighborly love, that we all must die, and that in this life, which we live only once, we have only one another. Smith's poem is set in the same season as Frost's, and employs the same imagery of neighbors and fences. But there are differences in argument even if they reach similar conclusions. Frost's poem tells of an active project between two neighbors who do not entirely understand each other. While there is no rational explanation as to why good fences should make good neighbors when there is nothing to keep in or out, the poem shows that participation in the ritual makes good neighbors. If fences don't make good neighbors in themselves, the ritual mending of them does so. Crichton Smith's poem reaches a conclusion not so far from this, that the act of loving your neighbor is the recognition of a common fate.

The neighbor we are called upon to love may be on a city street, across a river, or even within ourselves. This last possibility is evoked by W.H. Auden's elegy for Sigmund Freud. Freud died of cancer in September 1939, in London, 16 months after fleeing the Nazis, who had invaded his native Vienna the previous year. Auden, then 32 years old, had recently emigrated from England to the United States. He had been reading Freud since his university days, had wrestled with the psychoanalyst's theories on sexuality, and admired Freud's views on the psychology of art. Most importantly, his reading of Freud was part of his exploration of the nature of desire and of anxiety in the modern world. His reaction to the news of Freud's death was strong and immediate; his elegy appeared in the *Kenyon Review* in early 1940.

An elegy is a poem of mourning which commemorates the person, often a public figure, who has died. In this poem, Auden demonstrates Freud's greatness with an unusual degree of intimacy; he seeks to show why it is important not just to remember Freud but also to live in the light of his wisdom. As befits its subject, it is a substantial poem of 112 lines, but its argument can be grasped by considering its four main movements. In the first, the poet establishes the occasion of the poem: Freud's death at 80 at the beginning of the Second World War, "when there are so many we shall have to mourn." Freud is among those dead who had hoped to do some good for the world but who knew it was never enough: "still at eighty he wished To think of our life." But his death disappointed the "shades that still waited to enter the bright circle of his recognition," the many who in their suffering looked to him in hope of relief.

The second movement of the poem explains Freud's method in simple but eloquent terms. Freud, the poem says, merely had the Present recite the Past until, as in a poetry lesson, it hesitated at the place where

> Long ago the accusations had begun,
> And suddenly knew by whom it had been judged,
> How rich life had been and how silly,
> And was life-forgiven and more humble.

The poetry lesson is the effort to recite a poem by memory, and memory is the key to Freud's method: he wanted his patients to recite their pasts in complete candor. His "talking cure," then, consists of the story one tells about one's own life in an effort to locate the place where things went wrong, in order to forgive oneself. It is a humbling experience which nonetheless enables one to approach life anew "as a friend," without pretension and artifice. It is here that Auden evokes Freud's devotion to those who suffer, to the "Lost People" in the stinking ditch "where the injured Lead the ugly life of the rejected." The lost and injured are victims of an internal ill, that of denial—the denial of impulse, of love, of trauma. It is a form of repression equal in the damage it causes on a psychic level to the political oppressions of Freud's own day. Auden sees not just an analogy between psychic repression and political oppression, but also the real-world connection between the two, so that his language continually oscillates between them.

It is only logical, then, that the third movement of the poem should extend outward from Freud's practice to his importance in the world, which amounts to "a whole climate of opinion." Thanks to Freud we no longer think about our desire and our suffering in the same way. His influence extends from the highest levels of state, where he is mistrusted, to the "tired in even the remotest most miserable duchy," ordinary people who feel the change and are cheered. The final movement of the poem no longer speaks of Freud in the past tense; he is still present, and wishes for us more than the return of the long-forgotten objects of our memory. He wishes to unite the divided and unequal parts of ourselves, male and female, child and adult; he "would give back to The son the mother's richness of feeling."

The concluding lines of the poem are among the most powerful in modern poetry, in their sadness, their wisdom, and their faint glimmer of hope. They say that, above all, Freud would have us "be enthusiastic" over the night, because it needs our love. The night so pictured is inhabited by sad creatures—those of our hidden desires and impulses—who look to us to lead them out of the darkness. They are exiles who would rejoice if allowed, like Freud himself, to serve enlightenment. The poem concludes:

> One rational voice is dumb. Over his grave
> the household of Impulse mourns one dearly loved:
> sad is Eros, builder of cities,
> and weeping anarchic Aphrodite.

Auden wants us to welcome the night rather than just accept it, because its creatures, like those sorrowful ghosts in mythology, long for contact with us. Innocent in themselves, they transgress laws unknown to them. Thus condemned, they live in darkness as objects of repression. As figures of inarticulate impulse they cannot speak, but in their eyes we can see their desire to follow us, to be recognized as part of us, to be allowed to live in the light.

They would even, like Freud himself, bear the cry of "Judas," the revilement of so-called right-minded people, if that were the price of serving enlightenment, as Freud has done. Freud's voice now, like that of those seductive creatures, is silenced. But the household of Impulse mourns him. Auden draws on Greek mythology to name the creatures of Impulse, thereby lending them substance. The Greeks knew how to worship them. Auden reminds us that Eros is a figure for creative power as well as love, and that its power was once the energy behind the building of cities. Aphrodite represents another kind of love, that of sexuality, "anarchic" in its impulses, but now bereft of its chief defender in the modern age. These figures of impulse are the neighbors who live within us, in a place apart from our reason. They need our love and, as Auden conveys to us through the example of Freud, we need them for our own wholeness and enlightenment. This principle applies to all of the poems considered in this chapter: Whitman with the slaves and prostitutes, Frost with his country neighbor, Crichton Smith with his. In each case, the love of neighbor becomes a fulfillment of the soul's possibility.

Notes

1 Immanuel Kant, *Lectures on Ethics*, translated by Louis Infield, forward by Lewis White Beck. New York: Harper & Row, Publishers, Inc., 1963, p. 449.
2 C.S. Lewis, *God in the Dock : Essays on Theology and Ethics*, 1970.

Forgiveness

The act of forgiving has its origins in the nature of both contractual and moral obligations. In forgiving a debt we renounce any claim to be repaid, and in forgiving an offense we cease to harbor resentment and so relieve the offender of any need to make amends. These two objects of forgiveness are so intimately related in Western tradition that they occur in alternate versions of the Lord's Prayer. In Matthew 6, the prayer to the Father is to "forgive us our debts" (*opheilemata*), while in Luke 11 it is to "forgive us our sins" (*hamartias*). In both cases, forgiveness depends on the willingness of the one asking for forgiveness to forgive in turn. The quality of mercy is so important to the just conduct of human relations that not to forgive when there are grounds to do so can be an offense in itself. We ask forgiveness of God, of our parents, of our lovers, and even of ourselves. The act of forgiving belongs not only to the realms of religion, the law, and exchange; it can also be the result of profound introspection and of what Sigmund Freud called the "working through" of feelings of guilt and resentment. Our lives are lived in and through our relations with others, relations which often impose the need to be forgiven as well as the need to forgive.

In poetry as in life, forgiveness can take many forms, so that poets show us, in a variety of situations, how to ask for forgiveness. Something about the poetic vocation puts the poet usually in the position of asking for rather than granting forgiveness. Perhaps this is because poetic language itself is a kind of transgression against the habitual way of seeing and saying. By sayings things that have not been said before, the poet disturbs conventional modes of understanding. Or perhaps poets are inclined to ask forgiveness because this is one of the conditions of being human: how often do we live up to our own ideals, or to the expectations of others?

In English poetry, the classic appeal for forgiveness takes place in a religious context, where the poet prays for God's mercy. This is the case in one of John Donne's "divine" poems, "A Hymn to God the Father." The poem proceeds by seeking forgiveness for a series of no less than five sins belonging to the poet's past and present. There is first the original sin which belongs to human nature itself; then there is some unnamed sin which the poet commits in his present life, though he deplores it. He has further sinned by leading others into sin, and then there is another unnamed sin he has avoided for a year or two, but in which he "wallowed" for twenty years. For each of these sins in turn, once it has been forgiven by God there is "more" for him to forgive. The poet's sense of the number, the gravity, and the persistence of his sins is in fact one of the conditions of forgiveness, for in order to be forgiven one must be both conscious of and contrite for one's transgressions.

But there is a final sin which the poet must name, because he needs God's help in overcoming it. This is the sin the forgiveness of which is most difficult of all: the poet's fear of death, and the fate of his soul after death. He is afraid of perishing on "the shore" from which only the saved are ferried to paradise. Is it sin to fear death and the loss of one's soul? To Donne's way of thinking it is, in the sense that to have such fear amounts to a failure to trust God's mercy. The appeal to God in this last instance, however, is original with Donne:

> But swear by thyself, that at my death thy Son
> Shall shine as he shines now.

The poet asks God to promise that at the poet's death, God's son will continue to shine on the world, just as, like the sun, He shines now, giving life and hope to those below. This appeal is ingenious, in that while the poet needs forgiveness for the sin of fear, he asks God not to forgive it but rather to nullify it by removing the cause of fear. In effect, he asks God for a sign. In the closing lines of the poem the poet's prayer appears to have been answered:

> And, having done that, thou hast done;
> I fear no more.

The final words are given in the present tense, not the future conditional. This is not because God has "sworn" his constancy in a way not recorded in the poem. Rather, the act of prayer itself, which can only be valid on the condition of one's faith in God, has removed the poet's fear by reconfirming his faith. The power of the hymn is that it fulfils the object of its desire by means of its own performance.

Donne was a clergyman in the Church of England in the early seventeenth century. Except for the fact of original sin and his fear of death, we cannot know the nature of the other sins to which he refers in the poem. He does not so much confess them, which would require naming them more precisely, as ask whether forgiveness is forthcoming. It is as if full confession were not necessary, given God's knowledge of them. This is further evidence of the poet's faith that he believes God knows his transgressions intimately.

Note that Donne calls this poem a hymn rather than a prayer, both of which can take the form of verse. A hymn is a song of praise, which by its very nature expresses faith in the object of its praise. Donne's poem, which begins with a series of questions, thus saves its quality as a hymn only at the last moment, in its triumphant last words: "I fear no more." But in their testimony to God's power to remove the poet's fear, these words are praise enough. Donne's poem was set to music by the young English composer Pelham Humphry, who published it in his book of sacred songs in 1688. It continues to be performed today.

Donne's forgiveness depends on his faith in a merciful Deity beyond our world and the constraints of human relations: a God all-powerful and all-forgiving. Among us here below, forgiveness can be fraught with human frailty and thus is less assured. It is as if in modern life we no longer needed God's forgiveness but rather that of each other and ourselves. One of Emily Dickinson's poems frames her devotion to another person in terms of a natural allegory, that of the daisy and the sun.

> The daisy follows soft the sun,
> And when his golden walk is done,
> Sits shyly at his feet.
> He, waking, finds the flower near.
> Wherefore, marauder, art thou here?
> Because, sir, love is sweet!
>
> We are the flower, Thou the sun!
> Forgive us, if as days decline,
> We nearer steal to Thee,—
> Enamoured of the parting west,
> The peace, the flight, the amethyst,
> Night's possibility!

Between 1858 and 1862, Dickinson wrote passionate letters to someone she addressed as "Master." In these letters she refers to herself as "Daisy," more than once in appeal for forgiveness for some unnamed offense. The letters were found after her death, and it is not known whether they were ever sent, or to whom. However, similar letters are written to Samuel Bowles, editor of the *Springfield Republican* newspaper, a friend of the Dickinson family whom Emily met at her sister's house in 1858. "The daisy follows soft the sun" was written in 1860. The biographical evidence is that even if Dickinson conceived a passion for Bowles, he, a married man, did not return it, though he remained a close friend until his death in 1878. It has been conjectured that the Master and Bowles are one and the same person.[1]

Dickinson's poem follows a myth from Ovid: the nymph Clytie, enamored of the sun god Apollo, perished for love of him. She was transformed into a sunflower, which bends its face to follow the course of the sun from morning to night. The poem replaces the sunflower with the more common daisy, who follows the sun shyly until he asks the meaning of her intrusion. Her answer, "Because, sir, love is sweet!" is echoed by a letter Dickinson wrote to Bowles in 1862 beginning, "If I amazed your kindness—My Love is my only apology," adding later, "Forgive the Gills that ask for Air, if it is harm—to breathe!"[2]

The second verse shifts from the third to the first person, using the plural "we" which Dickinson often uses for her poetic self, who addresses the sun with the familiar "thee." She asks forgiveness for stealing closer to him in the evening, as if her closeness were burdensome to him. The excuse she offers, however, is more ambiguous. Here she confesses to being enamored not exactly of the sun, but of the effects of the sun's setting: "The peace, the flight, the amethyst, Night's possibility!" On Bowles's death in 1878, Dickinson wrote to his widow that when the sky over the neighboring hills turned purple on midwinter days, "we say 'Mr Bowles's colors.' " She adds an allusion to the "Gem chapter" of Revelation, where amethyst figures among the precious stones adorning the Holy City (Rev. 21:20). As if yearning for the possibilities of another world, the speaker of Dickinson's poem wants to follow the object of desire beyond her earth-bound existence into the shining mysteries of the night. The grounds on which she seeks forgiveness are thus not her devotion to the sun in the person of her "sir," but rather her aspiration to a realm beyond life as she knows it. Implicitly, she asks the person she follows to recognize the higher order of this realm, and to forgive the speaker's attachment to him as her introduction to it.

The appeal to a higher order is also the subject of another poem asking forgiveness, this time of those who might read Dickinson's work. In one of her best-known poems, she seeks the merciful judgment of her fellow countrymen:

> This is my letter to the world,
> That never wrote to me,—
> The simple news that Nature told,
> With tender majesty.
> Her message is committed
> To hands I cannot see;
> For love of her, sweet countrymen,
> Judge tenderly of me!

There is daring in writing to a public that never asked to hear from you. The poet acknowledges this in the first two lines, but seeks to excuse herself on the grounds that she is only conveying the news told to her by Nature. She therefore acts as an intermediary between Nature, which communicates with her, and the human world, which does not. The simplicity of the poem's language would seem to match the simplicity of the tale it transmits, but there are subtleties hidden within this claim. The "news" of Nature, combined with the tender majesty of that figure, cannot but recall the "good news" of Christ's coming as transmitted by the writers of the Gospel (Luke 9.6).

This allusion is not Dickinson's only appropriation of the religious tradition. Her poem is written in the "common meter" (alternating lines of four and three stresses) used in the hymns sung in the Congregational Church she attended with her family in Amherst. Her work thus stands as a modest rival, or at least an adjunct, to that august tradition, which is all the more reason for her to fear its reception. The risk she takes is heightened by the fact that she can know neither who will read her work nor how they will understand it. She therefore pleads for clemency in advance. There is flattery in addressing her readers as "sweet countrymen"; she points out that they inhabit the same natural landscape from which she draws her inspiration, and suggests that their love for it will soften their judgment in accordance with their "sweet" dispositions. To judge her "tenderly," moreover, would be in the spirit of Nature's "tender majesty." Such clemency would also forgive what she considers her temerity in writing to a world that never wrote to her. There are other reasons, however, for which Dickinson might seek forgiveness, from herself if not from others. The year after "This is my letter to the world," she wrote "Publication—is the Auction," a poem condemning publication as a tawdry sale of the mind, and claiming poverty as a just alternative. If she craves mercy for her letter to the world, then some of that mercy must come from herself.

This poem was written in about 1862, when Dickinson first began to correspond with Thomas Wentworth Higginson, a writer and Unitarian minister who had just published a "Letter to a Young Contributor" in the *Atlantic Monthly* offering practical advice to aspiring writers. At that time, Dickinson, aged 31, had published only five poems in local newspapers (including Bowles's *Springfield Republican*) over a period of twelve years, and these publications were anonymous. Her life in Amherst, though lived among intelligent and well-meaning persons, afforded little opportunity for her to judge the literary value of her work. She therefore sent four poems to Higginson with a brief letter which begins, "Are you too deeply occupied to say if my Verse is alive?" This letter began a correspondence which lasted until Dickinson's death in 1886. Higginson did not actively help Dickinson to publish her verse, but he encouraged her to write, and in 1890 he published the first edition of her poems. This edition included "This is my letter to the world," not published during the poet's lifetime. Her countrymen have indeed judged tenderly of Dickinson, because her verse is in fact alive. It has its source in the deepest well-springs of her being, where individual feeling is at one with something universal in human nature. There is admittedly a certain disproportion in comparing her plea for mercy at the hands of the public to Donne's prayer for God's forgiveness. But the two poets have in common an honesty based on self-knowledge. Dickinson's letter to Higginson, claiming she has no one else to ask, implores him to "tell me what is true." But her poems, however whimsical or despairing, are invariably made of the truth of herself and of her relation to nature. In this way her letter to the world, like Donne's hymn, justifies her appeal and the world's clemency in advance. The lesson here is that self-knowledge is a condition of forgiveness, first of oneself and then in the eyes of others.

We ask forgiveness of those to whom we are indebted—God, the world, those we love—because we are afraid not to have lived up to their expectations or to have justified their trust. In a traditional world that values family ties, poets tend to assert their independence. In a modern world that values "worldly" achievement, poets are notoriously impractical. In both cases, they can be susceptible to the feeling of not having lived up to the mark. Whether traditional or modern, in a patriarchal society this susceptibility is especially true of male poets, and is one reason for the number of poems by sons asking forgiveness of their fathers.

In 1914, William Butler Yeats, at the age of 48, had published five slender volumes of poetry in the dreamlike mode of the Irish Literary Revival. He was yet to become the international figure of his later years. The publication of a new book of poems, *Responsibilities*, however, marked a new phase in his work. The poet of "eternal beauty wandering on her way" turned to the more pressing concerns of the Ireland of his day, with a sparer, more incisive language. The concept of responsibility, with its duties to family, society, and nation, was also new to Yeats' poetry. The new collection of poems was initially published by the Cuala Press, a private concern in the town of Dundrum devoted to the Irish Revival and managed by Yeats's sister Elizabeth. But in 1916, the book was taken up by the London publisher Macmillan, giving it the wider audience which Yeats's work was to address thereafter. The book bears a preface in the form of 22 lines of iambic verse in which the poet addresses his male ancestors. It begins, "Pardon, old fathers, if you still remain Somewhere in ear-shot for the story's end [...]"

These opening lines suggest that the poet's "old fathers" may have already given up on him as having lived a wasted life. He nonetheless invokes them one by one: Benjamin Yeats, an eighteenth-century Dublin merchant whose trade was free of tariff duties; John Yeats, a pastor in Sligo who knew the Irish patriot Robert Emmet; the Butlers and Armstrongs who defeated the deposed King James II in the Battle of the Boyne in 1690; Robert Middleton, a trader and adventurer. In Yeats's eyes, these are all men of honorable character and accomplishment who have left him blood "that has not passed through any huckster's loin."

But most of all he addresses his maternal grandfather, William Pollexfen, a ship-owner with whom Yeats spent his summers as a boy in Sligo, and who gave his sanction to "wasteful virtues" such as imagination:

> You most of all, silent and fierce old man,
> Because the daily spectacle that stirred
> My fancy, and set my boyish lips to say,
> 'Only the wasteful virtues earn the sun';
> Pardon that for a barren passion's sake,
> Although I have come close on forty-nine,
> I have no child, I have nothing but a book,
> Nothing but that to prove your blood and mine.

The product of an Anglo-Irish family in the Victorian era, Yeats shared with others of his time and class a desire to perpetuate the family name. But in middle age he had yet to marry or to produce an heir, a circumstance he attributes here to his "barren passion," an allusion to his unrequited love for the actress and Irish nationalist Maud Gonne. He therefore asks pardon of his ancestors, all of whom are dead by now, for not having fathered a child. Notably absent from this heroic catalogue is the poet's father, John Butler Yeats, an artist then living in New York. The elder Yeats was not prolific in his work, and his son considered that he had ruined his career through "infirmity of will."[3] The more honored men of Yeats's ideal genealogy do not suffer from such weakness. To them he offers his book in place of an heir, as proof that the blood in his veins is the same that flowed in theirs.

The image of blood is important to the poem. In the case of Yeats's family line, for it not to have passed through any "huckster's loin" connects blood to the act of procreation. In the final line of the poem, however, ancestral blood is more a question of character. Yeats wants to be seen, or rather to see himself, as sharing the qualities of the men whose spirits he has just addressed: each one of them is recalled as having at least one of the qualities of worldliness, adventurousness, generosity, learning, honesty, courage, or wisdom. If Yeats's slender volume of 55 pages is offered to show what he has in common with all of that, there is reason for the diffidence of the poem's conclusion: "nothing but a book." Yet the book's title reflects Yeats's intention to meet his responsibilities, and its contents give voice to a maturer style than he has shown before, to a "sterner conscience" and a new militancy in defense of the arts against the provincial ignorance and venality of his countrymen. The erstwhile poet of youthful love and beauty declares himself ready to assume a role in the public sphere, to become the poetic voice of a newly emerging Irish national identity. In so doing, he hopes to prove himself—to prove to himself—that he is a worthy heir of the brave and wise generations from which he is descended. His pardon must come from his own work.

Yeats was briefly acquainted with another Irishman equally attentive to his place in family history. Throughout the many changes of residence in his life, James Joyce held on to a collection of family portraits which he proudly displayed to visitors. A coat of arms attributed to the Joyces of Galway likewise was carried from one place to another, as if to compensate for the uprooted existence of the writer's family. Unlike Yeats at 48, Joyce had a son and daughter when he was that age, and a grandson before he was 50. But he has other reasons for needing the forgiveness of his father. When Joyce's grandson was born in February 1932, six weeks after the death of Joyce's father, he wrote the following poem, entitled "Ecce Puer":

> Of the dark past
> A child is born;
> With joy and grief
> My heart is torn.

> Calm in his cradle
> The living lies.
> May love and mercy
> Unclose his eyes!
>
> Young life is breathed
> On the glass;
> The world that was not
> Comes to pass.
>
> A child is sleeping:
> An old man gone.
> O, father forsaken,
> Forgive your son!

If the poets of Donne's generation prayed to be forgiven by God the Father, poets like Yeats and Joyce need to be forgiven by their own fathers.

Joyce's poem, however, is not without religious echoes. Its title, meaning "Behold the child," echoes the words of the Vulgate version of Matthew 12:18, where Jesus echoes the prophet Isiaiah: "Ecce puer meus."—literally, "behold my child," the words of the Lord in designating the one whom he loves and whom he has chosen to "show judgment to the Gentiles." Joyce's title also resonates with the words Jesus addresses to his mother as he is taken to be crucified: "ecce filius tuus"—behold thy son (John 19:26). The poem's cadence of two-stresses per line reinforces the calm simplicity of the immediate scene, in contrast to the poet's conflicted feelings. The "dark past" out of which the child is born no doubt alludes to the death of the poet's father. For the birth of his grandson to follow so closely on this death accounts for Joyce's mixture of joy and grief. From this confessional mode the poet directs his attention to the child itself, calm in his cradle as the living being whose eyes will be unclosed, in contrast to the father whose eyes would have been closed at the moment of his death.

Let us forgive the poet for omitting all reference to the child's mother, Helen Kastor Joyce, or to his own mother, May Joyce. Like Yeats, Joyce grew up in the Victorian age, when traditional genealogy gave precedence to the male line of descent. In any case, Joyce is less interested in genealogy than Yeats was. As a poet he celebrates not just the birth but also the new life as creation, as the advent or "coming to pass" of a world which was not, which did not exist before now. Joyce thus composes a secular version of the biblical nativity, which announces a new life for humankind. The difference between Christ's nativity and this birth is the exclusively human nature of the latter: Joyce finds the sacred in the human moment, the everyday, the here and now. The conclusion of the poem turns from the sleeping child in order to address the poet's father directly: "O, father forsaken, Forgive your son!"[4] Joyce again borrows language from the crucifixion story, when Christ asks his Father to forgive his persecutors, "for they know not what they do" (Luke 23:34) and, a few moments later, when he asks the Father, "why has thou forsaken me?" (Matthew 27:46). In Joyce's appeal, however, it is his father whom *he* has forsaken, and of whom he asks forgiveness. The archives of the Zurich James Joyce Foundation have the typescript of a French translation Joyce made of the poem in 1940. He ends it with the words, "Père délaissé, De moi pitié"—Father abandoned, Have pity on me! The translation shows that Joyce cared enough about the poem to return to it eight years later, making the French version even more intimate by using the first person "moi" for the more impersonal "your son."

Joyce's letters are confirmation of the fact that he suffered deep feelings of remorse at his father's death. John Stanislaus Joyce died in Dublin when James Joyce was living in Paris. He had not seen his father since his last visit to Ireland in 1912. Nearly 20 years had passed. The year before his father's death, Joyce received a letter from a Dublin neighbor who had seen John Joyce in a sorry state. The letter said of him, "He is still of opinion that you alone care for him, and believe in him, and his whole thoughts are centred on your coming over so that he may see you before he dies."[5] This must have been heart-rending to Joyce, who nonetheless still put off a journey to Ireland. Three days after his father's death, Joyce wrote to T.S. Eliot,

> He had an intense love for me and it adds anew to my grief and remorse that I did not go to Dublin to see him for so many years. I kept him constantly under the illusion that I would come and was always in correspondence with him but an instinct I believed in held me back from going, much as I longed to. (January 1, 1932)

He wrote in the same vein to his patron, Harriet Shaw Weaver, "I knew he was old. But I thought he would live longer. It is not his death that crushed me so much but self-accusation" (January 17, 1932).

We can only guess at the instinct that kept Joyce away from his father; Joyce himself does not seem to know. We do know that Joyce owed a great deal to his father, whose language and personality provided much of the material for Joyce's fiction, where the elder Joyce figures in the character of Simon Dedalus. It is possible that Joyce felt overpowered in the actual presence of his father, and that an instinct for survival kept him at a distance, just as his father's portrait in a fictional character marked a distance from the old man himself. However that may be, the birth of the grandson crystallizes the poet's remorse: he asks forgiveness of his father for having forsaken him. Whereas in the case of the child, the poet has prayed that "love and mercy" would open his eyes, he now seeks that same mercy from his late father. In this emotional transaction, the newborn child is offered as propitiation to the poet's father for his transgressions. We ask pardon of the dead because we have not fulfilled our obligations to them, or because we have failed to live up to the example they set for us. But can the dead forgive? Joyce prays to a ghost; he can only imagine his father's forgiveness, and that cannot be enough. In his father's absence, the poet therefore can only seek some means of forgiving himself. The child's birth may help him to do so in some measure. Surely it also helps to temper grief with joy, and to put the appeal in words, which is always the first step toward being forgiven.

When Joyce tells Eliot that an instinct held him back from visiting his father, he testifies to the fact that the need for forgiveness can come from the feeling of not having given ourselves to others. But what if such withholding were necessary to keep ourselves whole, to be in fact who we are? The tension between the integrity of the self and the fear of solitude is at the heart of Stevie Smith's appeal in a poem called "Forgive Me." Smith (real name Florence Margaret Smith) was one of those poets whose outwardly conventional lives conceal a rich and intense inner experience. She lived in a dully respectable London suburb with her maiden aunt, she never married, and worked for 30 years as a secretary for a publisher of consumer magazines. Her secret life as a poet came to light when she was 35 with the publication of her first collection of verse, with its playful title, *A Good Time Was Had by All* (1937). Included was "Forgive me," a poem whose singing rhythm and childlike rhymes do little to conceal a sense of loneliness. Though raised in the Church of England, Smith was at best ambivalent toward religion, so that it is difficult to read her poem as addressed to a forgiving God. The need for forgiveness is no less powerful for all that.

The poem sets forth the urgency of the case by pleading, "Forgive me forgive me." Unmarried and without a lover, she asks pardon for never having given her heart away. She explains that her heart is her own, even if she would not wish to keep it alone forever. It is a paradoxical yet logical desire: cannot one retain possession of one's heart while also loving another? In any case, men frown on her; her refusal to give her heart has provoked resentment and disapproval. Smith writes at a time when unmarried women approaching middle age were often objects of ridicule or contempt. She thus writes as a woman, aware that the world does not approve of a woman her age who has never found love.

After stating the case that "my heart is my own," the poet moves to her past, and makes a key distinction between love and fancy. She admits to having thought that she loved, but her heart remained unmoved; it was only fancy. Love alone could move her heart, however carelessly her fancy roved. The absence of a lover, or even of a friend, is stated more directly at the end, which moves back to the present. The final image is the most striking of the poem:

> Forgive me forgive me for here where I stand
> There is no friend beside me no lover at hand
> No footstep but mine in my desert of sand.

Alone in an emotional desert, the poet is left without consolation and seemingly without forgiveness. Like Dickinson, she has asked pardon from the world at large, but with less hope for absolution.

However, does not the poem argue, with some reason, that there are grounds for forgiveness? The poet can hardly be blamed for not giving away a heart that stood unmoved. What is more, the final lines, like the plaintive tone of the poem as a whole, gives voice to the pain of loneliness from which she suffers. Surely we are more likely to forgive those who suffer from their own absence of love. Finally, her openness to love—"would I not keep it for ever alone"—is further reason to forgive her, if indeed forgiveness is needed. Once again, the argument of the poem creates the conditions for the forgiveness it seeks. In this way, it resembles other kinds of confessions: in religious ritual, the sincerity of confession and the depth of self-understanding it entails are sufficient grounds for the mercy of God. In psychoanalysis, these same qualities of authenticity and understanding enable the reconciliation with self that allows the individual to carry on with life. There is no evidence that Smith found love before her death in 1971. But an essay on religion she wrote in 1958 entitled "The Necessity of Not Believing" concludes with the words: "There is no reason to be sad. It is a good thing."

The seriousness of the need for forgiveness has not prevented poets from treating it lightly. Indeed that need is so earnest and so universal that a little comic relief is sometimes welcome. William Carlos Williams, who can be serious when he wants to, has written the following poem in the manner of a note left on a kitchen table.

> This is just to say
> I have eaten
> the plums
> that were in
> the icebox
>
> and which
> you were probably
> saving
> for breakfast
>
> Forgive me
> they were delicious
> so sweet
> and so cold

Since its first publication in 1934, this poem has had an unlikely history. It is inscribed as a permanent installation on the outer wall of a building in The Hague, in a neighborhood of banks and fine eighteenth-century houses. It is recited in the 2016 film *Paterson* by Jim Jarmusch. Students have wondered why it is considered a poem at all. The answer is that it has something to say, in the economy, precision, imagery, and feeling of poetic language. The line breaks also help, and they are not arbitrary: each has a single stress, and carves out a single image as the object of attention: "the plums"—the plosive and labial sounds of the word evoke the juicy things themselves.

Like many of Williams's poems, it recalls a domestic scene from his life in Rutherford, New Jersey, where he practiced medicine as a family doctor. We can assume that the person addressed in the poem is Flossie, his wife of 22 years. The title of the poem, which forms the introductory clause of the first sentence, is transparent in its attempt to minimize the breach of trust which the poet has committed. The initial confession is straightforward and factual—"I have eaten the plums"—though it resonates ironically with the confession of original sin of Genesis 3:12, where Adam confesses, "I did eat." The speaker of the poem tells where he found the plums before he estimates the damage that has been done in depriving his wife of a breakfast she had probably looked forward to with some expectation. The capital letter beginning the third verse marks the beginning of a new sentence and the appeal for forgiveness.

The grounds of this appeal, however, are unabashed to the point of being brazen. When the enjoyment of the transgression—"so sweet and so cold"—is given as reason for the poet's absolution, it is as if, guilty of having eaten the plums, he wants to claim a more radical kind of innocence, that of the child who is not responsible for his actions. Perhaps he also appeals to his wife's love for him, and to the satisfaction she might take in his pleasure. It is a shrewd way of asking forgiveness: to seek complicity in the vicarious pleasure of transgression from the one in a position to forgive. The success of such a strategy, however, depends on the kind of love that forgives in advance, and on the vividness with which the poet can represent that pleasure.

Williams's little poem, for all its fame, has not escaped being the object of satire, as in these lines from among the "Variations on a theme by William Carlos Williams," published in 1962 by Kenneth Koch:

> I gave away the money that you had been saving to live on for the next ten years.
> The man who asked for it was shabby and the firm March wind on the porch was
>   so juicy and cold.

Koch was a sort of court jester to the New York school of young poets in the 1950s and 1960s. His variations on Williams's poem employ the classical technique of hyperbole, in each case exaggerating both the gravity of the crime and the inanity of the excuse. It remains, however, a clever critique of the original, by pointing out implicitly that forgiveness is not without its conditions, requiring contrition for what has been done, and a due regard for the victim of the offense. These are conditions that apply to the one seeking forgiveness, and not necessarily to the one in the power to grant it: the quality of mercy is under no such restraint. Let us then forgive the wickedness of Koch's satire, because the laughter he evokes anticipates the joy of being forgiven.

Notes

1 See, for example, Judith Farr, *The Passion of Emily Dickinson*. Cambridge, MA: Harvard University Press 1992.
2 Emily Dickinson, *Letters*, ed. Thomas H. Johnson. Cambridge, MA: Harvard University Press, 1986, vol. 2, p. 393.
3 Letter to John Quinn, cited in Colm Toibin, "The Playboy of West 29th Street," *London Review of Books*, vol. 40, no. 2 (25 January 2018), pp. 7–12.
4 In order to avoid the typographical intrusion of the slash [/], line breaks are indicated by capital letters.
5 Letter from James Valentine Dunn to James Joyce, July 1, 1930. Courtesy of the Zurich James Joyce Foundation, with thanks to Harald Beck and Vincent Deane for their research in identifying the sender.

Finding the Center

Ralph Waldo Emerson believed that the laws of nature are moral laws, and that we can learn how to live by understanding and following nature: our own nature as well as that which is manifest in the forests and fields around us. "The moral law lies at the center of nature and radiates to the circumference," he writes in his essay *Nature*. Lyric poetry, especially since the Romantic era, tends to take place in the space of nature, and to organize that space around a center. The center also has figurative meaning. In the figure of the radiating center, Emerson calls on one of the fundamental structures of human existence: we organize our daily lives around a center of activity or interest, and even think of ourselves as having a central identity, which we name variously as the heart, the soul, the spirit, or mind: "the deep heart's core," in Yeats's words. In addition, the center is variously understood in relation to movement: as the point around which things revolve, from which things emanate, or toward which things tend.

The human relation to God has also been configured according to a spatial center. In the Book of Exodus, God calls for the making of a sanctuary, so that he may dwell in the midst of his people. Following this commandment, the priestly writer of chapter 25 gives the specifications for the tabernacle by moving from the center to the periphery—from the ark containing the word of God outward to the furnishings and court. The Christian tradition follows this basic design by placing the altar at the center of the church, at the intersection of nave and transept. The center is always the point of communion with God. The monastic tradition, for its part, has a contemplative practice known as the centering prayer: an inward concentration that frees the individual from distractions and clears a space for spiritual awareness. In recent years, this kind of contemplative practice has been adapted to secular and therapeutic purposes under names such as body-mind centering or mindfulness. This latter movement is aimed at stress reduction rather than spiritual enlightenment, but in its language the figure of the center remains, well, central.

Poets offer testimonies to finding the center that are both independent of traditional religious context and more lastingly meaningful than the techniques of stress reduction. The opening lines of a Wordsworth sonnet from 1802 describe the condition that makes spiritual centering necessary:

> The world is too much with us; late and soon,
> Getting and spending, we lay waste our powers;—
> Little we see in Nature that is ours;
> We have given our hearts away, a sordid boon!

Wordsworth finds that we have wasted the powers of our own nature on the mere business of getting on in the world. We have sacrificed what is of most value to that world, and received little in return. We remain strangers to Nature, in the nobler sense of its beauty and spiritual power.

In the same year, the poet finds solace from his condition at a seemingly chance moment in an unexpected place: the center of London, on the bridge between the north and south banks. Here are the lines "Composed upon Westminster Bridge, September 3, 1802":

> Never did sun more beautifully steep
> In his first splendour, valley, rock, or hill;
> Ne'er saw I, never felt, a calm so deep!
> The river glideth at his own sweet will:
> Dear God! the very houses seem asleep;
> And all that mighty heart is lying still!

Wordsworth puts the date of the poem in the title as if to mark the exceptional nature of this morning among others. But the date has another importance for his life. In September 1802, he had just returned from Calais, where he was briefly reunited with Annette Vallon, the mother of his child Caroline, now 9. He had not seen the child since the first year of her life. The poet was now engaged to his sister's friend, Mary Hutchinson. Amidst the tumult of emotions which these events must have produced in the poet, the deep calm recorded in the poem must have come as a moment of grace.

The opening lines of the sonnet define the beauty of the scene by means of a language of exception that eliminates other earthly scenes along with dull-minded men, while establishing direct contact between the present scene, "so touching in its majesty," and the poet's soul:

> Earth has not anything to show more fair:
> Dull would he be of soul who could pass by
> A sight so touching in its majesty:

The poem is spatially organized in two movements. The first of these moves centripetally from the horizon of the earth to the closer vision of the city in the clear air of dawn, before the chimney fires cloud it in smoke:

> This City now doth, like a garment, wear
> The beauty of the morning; silent, bare,
> Ships, towers, domes, theatres, and temples lie
> Open unto the fields, and to the sky;
> All bright and glittering in the smokeless air.

The silence and bareness of the scene allow an unusually clear perception of the city's built structures, distinguished by type and named sequentially as the poet looks around him: ships, towers, domes, theatres, temples.

In the concluding six lines, the connection between seeing and feeling is made more explicit, as if the clarity of the brightening September air enabled the poet to see within himself more clearly:

> Never did sun more beautifully steep
> In his first splendour, valley, rock, or hill;
> Ne'er saw I, never felt, a calm so deep!
> The river glideth at his own sweet will:
> Dear God! the very houses seem asleep;
> And all that mighty heart is lying still!

The poet's vision returns to the eastern horizon only to move further inward this time, to the seat of his profoundest feeling, where an inner peace coincides with the calm of the outer scene. A series of negatives systematically eliminates all previous experience in order to establish the unique nature of the present moment: "never" did sun more beautifully dawn on the land, "never" did the poet see, "never felt, a calm so deep." The river gliding beneath the poet's feet at its own sweet will is a figure of natural freedom released from outer constraint. It suits the poet's own sense of freedom in this moment of blessed stillness, felt not just in the world around him but equally in the depth of his own being. His voice bursts forth in a spontaneous prayer of thanksgiving. The moment has allowed the poet to find that place in himself that joins him with God and the earth.

Modern poetry is full of such moments of dynamic contemplation, where the mind moves from the outer landscape inward in a way that alters the poet's sense of self and of the world. T.S. Eliot's poem "Burnt Norton" is the first of the magisterial *Four Quartets*. As poetic compositions, the *Quartets* have the emotional complexity of Beethoven's late string quartets, after which they are named. "Burnt Norton" was first published in 1936, and signaled a newly contemplative direction in Eliot's work, which in poems like *The Waste Land* had been preoccupied with the chaos and spiritual emptiness of the modern world. The newly contemplative mode was in keeping with Eliot's decision to join the Church of England in 1927. "Burnt Norton" is an ode to the spiritual dimension of life inspired by his faith but expressed in a language having only an indirect relation to Christian doctrine and iconography. It is rather a series of reflections drawn from the poet's own thought and experience. It is serious and elevated in style, while not lacking in the humility befitting the poet's search for a truth that will ultimately transcend his understanding. In this respect, the poem has much in common with the great odes of Wordsworth and other poets of the Romantic period. The poem's title borrows the name of a seventeenth-century manor house in the Cotswolds which Eliot visited in 1934. The house was so named because it was built on the ruins of an earlier manor which had burned down. Eliot was visiting his friend Emily Hale in a nearby village, and the two of them discovered the house by accident. It was unoccupied and its gardens neglected. The atmosphere of decay, combined with Eliot's complex feelings about Emily, appears to have produced the profound effects to which the poem testifies.

The poem begins with a meditation on the nature of time, with particular emphasis on "what might have been." Eliot, now 46, had been in love with Emily when a young man at Harvard before the war. But he had gone off to England, had made a hasty, disastrous marriage with Vivienne Haigh-Wood, and had lost contact with Emily for many years. In 1934, Eliot was separated from Vivienne, but still married. His renewed friendship with Emily was more spiritual than romantic, and his life with her could be thought of only as what might have been. It is evoked in the poem as "the door we never opened Into the rose-garden." The poet nonetheless invites his companion into Burnt Norton's abandoned garden, through a gate and along an alley which opens onto a drained pool:

> And the pool was filled with water out of sunlight,
> And the lotos rose, quietly, quietly,
> The surface glittered out of heart of light.

The poet's path has moved inward through a series of concentric spaces to arrive at this point. In a combination of a simple natural phenomenon with poetic imagination, the empty, decayed pool, bathed in sunlight, is miraculously transformed into a luminous vision. The poet's inspiration has endowed the pool with the sacred lotus of Buddhist mythology. The flower rises to the glittering surface from what the poet calls the heart of light, a figure for the inner peace he seeks. This is the experience that is to redeem his past, including his lost love for Emily Hale, by transforming it into a spiritual ideal. It is not altogether unlike the moment on Westminster Bridge where Wordsworth's emotional losses are redeemed by another light.

But Eliot's sudden illumination is fleeting, so that the second movement of his poem engages in a more systematic intellectual formulation of his experience. Here the transitory light of the pool is replaced by the more abstract, and therefore more permanent image of the still point:

> At the still point of the turning world. Neither flesh nor fleshless;
> Neither from nor towards; at the still point, there the dance is,
> But neither arrest nor movement.

The still point lies at the center of the turning world, but it is not still in the sense of arrest or fixity. Like Wordsworth describing his moment of earthly beauty, Eliot must define the still point in terms of what it is not: neither flesh nor fleshless, from nor toward, ascent nor decline. Though it gathers past and future, it is not to be placed in time. Eliot does not call it the dance, but says that it makes the dance possible. The figure of the dance is traditional in poetry, though here it is unusually charged with meaning. Dance creates its own space and time, and thus can move independently of fixed measures of space and time. It has no goal beyond its own expression. It is also a movement of sublime fusion of the human body with artistic beauty, as Yeats famously implies when he asks, "How can we tell the dancer from the dance?" In Eliot's language, the dance is an ideal image for the world's movement around a point that is not *of* the world. It is a figure of transcendence captured in the movement of a human body. In like manner, Eliot's poem seeks to awaken a sense of that transcendent power out of the imperfect material of language.

The poet assures us that he has been present at the ideal place of convergence, though its position beyond earthly notions of time and place prevents him from saying where or when. In fact, he says that "we" have been there, and if his companion is Emily Hale, this could be an attempt to elevate the nature of their relation to something greater than the love between man and woman. Whatever the poet's purpose, the psychological and spiritual conditions of presence at the still point are defined in terms, drawn alike from Eastern and Western traditions, which stretch the limits of conceptual language. The poet has experienced a sense of freedom through release from the burdensome conditions of being—release from the practical desire for the things of this world, from action and suffering, from the compulsions we impose on ourselves, or have imposed on us from others. Eliot presents the detachment from such things not as an escape, but as a form of grace through which we can live in the world. Here the heart of light and the still point are brought together in the image of the "white light still and moving." In Eliot, this light is made the visual image of what he calls "a grace of sense."

Among the multiple meanings of "grace" are the aesthetic, related to the harmony and beauty of a being or a gesture, and the theological, as the benevolence of divine intervention. Both meanings are present in Eliot's use of the word, where we may take "sense" to refer to both sensory perception and human understanding, here united with the life of the spirit. The freedom from desire and the release from action are also the union of the poet's being with something greater than these things. Wordsworth's sonnet expresses a similar union in simpler but equally elevated terms, where the sight of the earth's majesty touches the poet's soul.

In Eliot's poem, the still point at the center finds its antithesis in a "place of disaffection" which is nothing less than the modern world itself: for Eliot as well as Wordsworth, the world is too much with us. In a phrase that proves prophetic for our contemporary media landscape, Eliot calls this the "twittering world." He evokes it in stark images of "Men and bits of paper, whirled by the cold wind," and unhealthy souls,

> Driven on the wind that sweeps the gloomy hills of London,
> Hampstead and Clerkenwell, Campden and Putney,
> Highgate, Primrose and Ludgate.

The names of London's gloomy hills evoke the stations on the Underground and the strained, time-ridden faces caught in the daily rounds of worldly care. William Blake's "London" registers a similar sight in 1789, as the poet wandering through the city streets "mark[s] with every face I meet Marks of weakness, marks of woe." In both poets, these are the conditions from which humankind needs to be saved. Eliot's own quest for a saving grace returns to the image of light:

> After the kingfisher's wing
> Has answered light to light, and is silent, the light is still
> At the still point of the turning world.

Here are combined once again silence and light, the transitory and the eternal, the presence at the center, recalling John's testimony that "the light shines in the darkness" (I:5). But Eliot does not insist on the religious meaning of his poem. The freedom he seeks is reached equally through a movement of enlightened contemplation.

Eliot's poem arrives at this place having begun with the invitation to enter the rose-garden, as if to recapture there an original innocence associated with his youthful passion for Emily Hale, and beyond that, with childhood. As it happens, the foliage is "full of children, Hidden excitedly, containing laughter." Eliot's spiritual journey thus entails both a movement inward toward the center and a movement back in time, toward a lost origin of innocence. In similar fashion, Frost's "Directive," published in 1947, invites us on a journey back in time that has its own centered destination. It begins with these lines:

> Back out of all this now too much for us,
> Back in a time made simple by the loss
> Of detail, burned, dissolved, and broken off
> Like graveyard marble sculpture in the weather,
> There is a house that is no more a house
> Upon a farm that is no more a farm
> And in a town that is no more a town.

The opening line echoes Wordsworth's "The world is too much with us; late and soon" in its austere sequence of ten monosyllables, and its expression of the need to turn away from a world of meaningless excess. Frost wrote this poem at a time when he had become an American icon, and the same volume in which "Directive" is published contains an ironic poem "On Being Idolized." But Frost was in his seventies, and had lost his wife and three of his children. In "Directive," the sense of loss takes form both in the image of the graveyard subjected to the violence of time, and in the memory of a world—house, farm, and town—that no longer exists. The graveyard monument itself is an image of the poet's memory "made simple by the loss Of detail" which the poem's story will nonetheless supply in the abundance of imagination.

The backward glance in time becomes in the poem a movement through space of the kind that Frost has used in other poems where the journey has no destination but to go further than the poet has been before. Likewise, the road to this place that no longer exists is shown by a guide, the poet himself, "who only has at heart your getting lost." In his conversational, meandering fashion, Frost directs us in time from the distant past forward to the present moment, and in space from the outer landscape to a place where two village cultures faded into each other, but

> Both of them are lost,
> And if you're lost enough to find yourself
> By now, pull in your ladder road behind you
> And put a sign up CLOSED to all but me,
> Then make yourself at home.

Here is the turning point in the poem, where loss is not extinction, but the condition of self-discovery. Similarly paradoxical, in Frost's sly wit, is the "home" the reader is invited to make among the ruins of houses no longer homes. Assured of the reader's exclusive attention, the poet pursues his journey in ever narrowing spheres: from ruined village to field, from there to a children's make-believe house with its broken playthings, then to what was once a family home:

> [...] the house that is no more a house,
> But only a belilaced cellar hole,
> Now slowly closing like a dent in dough.

The images of absence have reached their point of ultimate vacancy: the cellar hole is all that remains of the house, yet the hole itself is disappearing, so that finally no trace of human life will remain. The closing dent in dough recalls the homely life now absent from this forsaken place. Like Eliot's dry pool, Frost's hole is the topographic figure of the void at the center of the suffering soul. But in a final turn, the arrival at this place of emptiness turns out to be the condition for discovering the source of renewal in a nearby spring. Frost's vision is again like Eliot's in combining images of ruined excavation with flowers and water. Aware of the highly traditional nature of his image, Frost makes apologetic references to the stories of redemption in the Grail myth and in Mark's Gospel (8:35). Jesus's direction to his disciples to drink the blood of the covenant (Mark 14:24) are also echoed in the concluding lines of Frost's poem:

> Here are your waters and your watering place.
> Drink and be whole again beyond confusion.

Here as elsewhere, the poem follows a narrative that bears affinity with Christian journeys of the soul. But Frost is not a Christian poet, and his poem implies that the wholeness achieved is that of self-discovery—"if you're lost enough to find yourself"—rather than the discovery of God. It is a modern parable, where the way to wholeness is tortuous, through memory and through life on earth, from loss to utter emptiness. In its earlier stages, the poem has engendered a kind of formal confusion in its indirection, its garrulousness, its folksy asides and its details of doubtful relevance. There is thus a formal correspondence between Frost's language and the getting-lost that is the subject of the poem, and which is the only way to its destination. The watering place is at once center, source, and origin; the lines that disclose it come with the simple clarity of an authentic directive.

Taking the poems of Wordsworth, Eliot, and Frost together, we begin to see a certain constellation of motifs: the journey, the particular place at the center charged with meaning, stillness, light, and spirit. All of these are present in a poem by Theodore Roethke. "The Far Field" was the title poem of a volume published the year after Roethke's death in 1963. The poem is an extended lyric of the kind invented by Wordsworth: a personal meditation on the meaning of the poet's own life, inspired by the experience of a natural landscape. The poem's images of mountain, river and sea recall the landscape of Washington State in the Pacific Northwest, where Roethke spent his final years. But the poem is not specific to that place, any more than the experience it evokes, though deeply personal, is limited to the poet. The language of the poem alternates between figures of finality and infinity. In its contemplation of the landscape as a projection of the poet's self it reaches a center of being, then moves outward again like the widening ripples around a stone cast in the sea.

It begins, like Frost's poem, with a journey, or rather a series of dreamed journeys: of flying like a bat into a narrowing tunnel, or of driving alone out a long peninsula:

> The road changing from glazed tarface to a rubble of stone,
> Ending at last in a hopeless sand-rut,
> Where the car stalls,
> Churning in a snowdrift
> Until the headlights darken.

These are dreams of dying. The journeys are of solitude and finitude: the narrowing tunnel, the road less and less passable until it comes to a dead end, the progressive diminishment leading to the final extinguishing of the headlights.

The poem then shifts registers, from dream to memory. In what seems a youthful reminiscence of wandering the fields, the poet remembers animals he found dead "at the field's end": the dead rat, the blasted tom-cat, the young birds and rabbits caught in the mirror. But whatever he suffered from the sight of death brought abundant recompense: "one learned of the eternal." His grief was not excessive, because to come upon warblers in the spring made him forget time and death. He takes pleasure in naming them: "Cape May, Blackburnian, Cerulean." The brilliance and plenitude of life in all its sounds and colors dazzle him. The very names of the birds in all their variety are joyful to recite. Reflecting on his own common origin with the creatures of nature—"once I was something like this"—the poet remembers how he came to the belief that he could return to life as another creature, a bird or a lion. In so identifying with nature, the poet who had learned of the eternal also learned another lesson:

> I learned not to fear infinity,
> The far field, the windy cliffs of forever,
> The dying of time in the white light of tomorrow,
> The wheel turning away from itself,
> The sprawl of the wave,
> The on-coming water.

The fear he has overcome is that of death, here called infinity in the new understanding that death is simply part of the natural cycle of life. A series of images evokes this never-ending cycle. The far field replaces the earlier "field's end." Windy cliffs give out onto the sea; the dawn is ever-recurring; a wheel continues to turn; one wave is followed by another; the ocean water is always oncoming.

Expanding on this reflection, the poem now moves from memory to the present moment, in which the poet feels "a weightless change, a moving forward." He describes this feeling by means of an elaborate analogy with the flow of a river from mountain height through narrow rapids, and finally to an alluvial plain. Here the river slows down, like the poet's life in late middle age. Wild grapes overhang it, weeds grow on the banks inhabited by crabs, small snakes, and bloodsuckers. The poet sees in the river another metaphor for his life:

> I have come to a still, but not a deep center,
> A point outside the glittering current;

Roethke presents the by now familiar constellation of images at the center—stillness, water, glittering light—in his own way. In this case the center is still but not deep, like the river shallowing in the plain, so that the poet may remain part of what surrounds him. The forms of nature are an ever-present lesson in death and renewal unfolding before his eyes. He has learned the lesson, so that the thought of his own death renews him, and inspires his love for the things dying in his world: "What I love is near at hand, Always, in earth and air."

The last part of the poem evokes, as Frost does, the "lost self" that changes. Here that self takes the form of an old man by the sea, dressed in "garments of adieu," his spirit moving like the wind that becomes gentle on a sunny plateau: "He is the end of things, the final man," a kind of monument to human finitude. But the final man is also the ideal figure of the poet who sees past his own finitude into the infinitude of the world. "All things reveal infinitude": the shadow falling on the mountain, the blue light of snow, the odor of bass-wood or of bees,

> A ripple widening from a single stone
> Winding around the waters of the world.

In this intensely lyrical conclusion, Roethke turns away from mythic abstraction, returning to his repertoire of brilliant images as the way most "near at hand" to show the infinitude revealed by things that die. The sequence of images moves from mountain height to sea, calling upon various senses. Each image is one of stillness, so that together they compose the "pure serene of memory in one man." This is a refinement of the youthful memories evoked earlier in the poem. It is Roethke's final image of the center, where the man is compared to a single stone in the sea around which the ripples widen toward the waters of the world at large. The poem ends in this expansive gesture, one which characterizes the Whitmanesque energy of Roethke's language in its attempt to comprehend all things, including the rusted objects in the dump at the forgotten end of the field. Throughout its progress, the poem has moved inward to the limit of the poet's being, and then, through the transformation he calls learning, it has moved outward from this center to comprehend the vast and various world.

In this poem as in others, one has to make a journey to finally arrive at the center, so that the experience has the sense of an ending. This is also the case in Stevens's "Final Soliloquy of the Interior Paramour," written near the end of the poet's life, in 1950. A soliloquy is a speech given by an actor alone on the stage. The poem's title combines this idea of solitude with that of finality. The final soliloquy is not just the last; it is also the crowning moment, like the finale of an orchestral piece. The interior paramour is Stevens's fanciful name for a presence within the "central mind" with which the poet seeks communion. In a television documentary on Stevens produced in the 1980s, the poet James Merrill gave an emotional reading of this poem, which he followed by saying, "Sometimes I feel about this poem the way other people feel about the 23rd Psalm." One understands him. The psalm testifies to the restorative power of a presence to whom the psalmist says, "thou art with me; thy rod and thy staff they comfort me" (23:4). Stevens's poem is the response to that experience of a twentieth-century poet whose faith lies in the imagination, and whose poem addresses a being equally as reassuring to him as that addressed by the psalmist.

The poem combines formal elegance with simplicity in its six verses. It is also ordered symmetrically: the first three verses arrange the rendezvous between the poet and his interior paramour; the final three define its effects. Unlike the other poems we have seen in this chapter, this one takes place entirely inside, "as in a room." The moment is the lighting of "the first light of evening," where the poet and his inmost being are collected out of all their differences into a single being. In this intimate rendezvous is found "A light, a power, the miraculous influence." Stevens borrows from the language of scripture—light, power, miracle—for the poet's meeting with the inmost part of himself, where he and that presence are collected into one thing.

The difference between this meeting and Scripture is that in Stevens the ultimate good is not the object of religious belief in the traditional sense, but of imagination: "The world imagined is the ultimate good." It helps to know that Stevens understands imagination in the largest possible sense, as the creative power out of which human beings have created their world. Human imagination is not the product of a single mind, but rather of our collective, historical relation to the natural world and to one another. This includes the "ultimate good," the "interior paramour," and the poem itself. To say that these things are creations of the imagination does not diminish their power, their goodness, or their beauty. If, as the poet says, we think "for small reason" that the world imagined is the ultimate good, then that reason will nonetheless have to suffice. It is an act of faith found beyond reason, like that of the devout Christian. Stevens's poem thus recounts an act of imagination, where out of a world full of undifferentiated images something single and intense is made, the self is collected unto its ideal in itself, as within a tightly wrapped shawl. The "miraculous influence" comes from just this closeness, as it would in communion with God. The consequences of this ideal union are the subject of the concluding lines, where "We say God and the imagination are one":

> Out of this same light, out of the central mind,
> We make a dwelling in the evening air,
> In which being there together is enough.

The condition for this experience is "to forget each other and ourselves," to efface the boundaries that exist between the conscious self we present to the world and our inmost being. It is no longer here a question of the "indifferences" out of which the rendezvous is retrieved, but rather an inner union of "ourselves" within the one boundary that counts, the vital one of the mind. The intimate feelings of order, wholeness, and knowledge give way to a more philosophical statement: "We say God and the imagination are one …" This is a direct consequence of the earlier assertion that "the world imagined is the ultimate good," because for Stevens, God is the ultimate act of the imagination, and because the imagination takes the place of God in giving meaning, value, and beauty to reality. That "we say" limits the doctrinal force of the statement, and justly so, because the world itself is made by what we say and imagine, and because poetry is not doctrine.

Even so, the union at the heart of this poem is illuminated by an image made meaningful by faith: "How high that highest candle lights the dark." Like Eliot, Stevens calls on the evangelist's image: "the light shines in the darkness" (John I:5), the difference being that for Stevens, the light comes from a homely source, the candle, rather than from the divine, just as the imagination has its source in the human mind. The candlelight shining in darkness is one of several images with origins in Scripture which Stevens has adapted to the world of human imagination. In Scripture, the psalmist concludes his song with the conviction that "I will dwell in the house of the Lord for ever" (23:6). Stevens's conclusion also speaks of dwelling, a word which, because of its use in the King James Bible, has a spiritual resonance. Stevens's use of the word, however, has differences in nuance. There is the same sense of conviction as in King James, but rather than being the house of the Lord, the dwelling in Stevens's poem has to be made in the inner light of the mind.

Let us grant that neither the "central mind" nor the "interior paramour" corresponds to anything real in a concrete, objective sense. These things are imagined; they take form in language. But to paraphrase Yeats, what else is there to moralize our days out of their aimlessness? That Stevens's dwelling is made in the evening air, that it may not be there forever, is a consequence of its supremely fictional nature. Accordingly, the final statement assures us merely of a sufficiency rather than the overwhelming plenitude of a cup that runneth over: "being there together is enough." But enough, in this case, is much. Stevens is wise enough not to present himself as a prophet; his head is not anointed with oil. Yet his poem consecrates the achievement of all that can be imagined, where imagination is the highest good. For Stevens as for the other poets cited here, the center is not a place of solitude. It is where the poet finds something within—the interior paramour, the select society, the still point, God—from which everything radiates. Stevens has found the center, has found light and comfort there, and it is enough.

Humility

In an age that encourages self-promotion, humility is hardly considered a virtue. Yet it is one of the most ancient values of the Western tradition. The Book of Proverbs says, "A man's pride shall bring him low, but honour shall uphold the humble in spirit" (29:23). And the most famous verse from the Book of Micah names humility with justice and mercy as what God has shown to humankind as the good: "and what doth the Lord require of thee, but to do justly, and to love mercy, and to walk humbly with thy God?" (6:8). Perhaps surprisingly, I want to make a connection between humility and the contemplative act of finding the center discussed in the previous chapter. In the tradition of the centering prayer, what is found at the center is not the self as such, but the presence of God. The one who prays can receive God into himself or herself, but God remains radically other than the self. Even in the secular poetic tradition, the inmost being toward which the centering movement tends is not the self of self-promotion, the self we present to the world. Stevens speaks of the interior paramour as a kind of companion, and insists throughout on the plural "we," as if to make clear that the act of communion requires two distinct beings. Finding the center, then, is not a narcissistic act, but rather the act of going beyond the self as mere self-presentation. Nor is humility in its purest form a negative quality. There is no question here of the paralyzing, destructive mode of self-accusation in which one finds comfort in the superiority of the accuser even while being shamed as the accused. Rather, true humility is a form of freedom; it transcends the self in the recognition that one's self is the other in the other's eyes. More than this, the quality of humility recognizes, as Roethke does, the finitude of the self in the face of infinity. The philosopher Emmanuel Levinas writes, "The idea of infinity implies a soul capable of containing more than it can take from itself."[1] Humility, then, is the quality of knowing that the world is much greater than oneself, and that one matters to others only insofar as one finds meaningful forms of relation with them. To the biblical injunction to walk humbly with thy God, poets have added a complex human dimension. We must walk humbly with our fellow human beings in an imperfect world. Humility's contrary, pride, is an obstacle to understanding, as Alexander Pope writes in the *Essay on Criticism* (1711). Pope's verse "essay" is intended as advice to critics. The qualities of good judgment are central to his message. But since judgment and "good sense" are also essential qualities in life, his lessons apply to more than the practice of criticism. In Part II of the poem, Pope examines the reasons for error in judgment, the chief of which is personal pride, as it obscures the light of truth. Pride is the "vice of fools," it blinds us to our faults, like a cloud that obscures the light of the sun.

> If once right reason drives that cloud away,
> Truth breaks upon us with resistless day;
> Trust not yourself; but your defects to know,
> Make use of ev'ry friend—and ev'ry foe.

Pride here is not just an obstacle. It leads to error and fills the void left by lack of sense, just as "wind" fills those parts of the body not made of blood or the spirit. Only if the cloud of pride is dispelled by right reason, meaning reason in the service of justice, can truth break upon us like the light of the sun. In what may seem a surprising alliance, truth is made the consequence of humility, for the light of truth shines only when pride is banished. The concluding lines of this excerpt are a prescription for humility: do not trust yourself, but know your defects. Make use not just of your friends, but of your enemies; they can show you where you are wrong. Humility is a devotion to truth.

Such devotion can also take the form of reverence for the lowliest and commonest things of life, a reverence manifested by Whitman throughout his *Song of Myself*. One passage of that poem is particularly illustrative. In it, a child comes to the poet with a question difficult to answer:

> A child said, What is the grass? fetching it to me with full hands;
> How could I answer the child? ... I do not know what it
> is any more than he.
>
> I guess it must be the flag of my disposition, out of hopeful
> green stuff woven.
>
> Or I guess it is the handkerchief of the Lord,
> A scented gift and remembrancer designedly dropped,
> Bearing the owner's name someway in the corners, that we
> may see and remark, and say Whose?
>
> Or I guess the grass is itself a child ... the produced babe
> of the vegetation.
>
> Or I guess it is a uniform hieroglyphic,
> And it means, Sprouting alike in broad zones and narrow zones,
> Growing among black folks as among white,
> Kanuck, Tuckahoe, Congressman, Cuff, I give them the
> same, I receive them the same.
>
> And now it seems to me the beautiful uncut hair of graves.
> (from part 6)

The figure of the child itself is one of simple innocence, and his full hands are a sign of abundance. His question, "What is the grass?" is really the question of what life is, and of what life means. The question itself, however, elicits a confession of ignorance, a sign of humility on the poet's part: "I do not know what it is any more than he."

The series of guesses which follows avoids, as guesses do, any conclusion as to the true meaning of the grass. Instead, they reflect the poet's wonder at the beauty and variety of creation. He begins with what is closest at hand; his own disposition or character is "out of hopeful green stuff woven." Whitman recovers the tradition, in medieval Christianity as elsewhere, of green as the color of hope and renewal. He suggests that the texture of his disposition, like the text of his poem, is "woven" out of this simple everyday stuff. The second guess is more playful, but in like fashion it treats the grass as a sign: a scented handkerchief "designedly" dropped by the Lord to remember him by, and marked somewhere in the corner by the owner's name. Whitman suggests, first, that our wonder at the beauty of nature is part of God's design; second, that his mark or signature is to be found "someway in the corners," in out of the way places we would not expect to find it, where, remarking but not recognizing it, we say, whose?

The search for the meaning of the grass does not end with this theological explanation. Faced with the child's question, Whitman can equally entertain the thought that the grass itself is a child, "the produced babe of the vegetation," implying a kinship between verdant nature and human generation: nature gives birth to its own children, including both the grass and the questioning child. Though this is a genial connection between the two things nearest at hand, the poet remains tempted by the idea of the grass as a sign of something greater. Thus, he entertains the idea that the grass is a "uniform hieroglyphic," covering the landscape in its differing contours, and growing without distinction among the various races, regional peoples, and classes of North America. Hieroglyphic is Greek for "sacred writing," a form of communication reserved in antiquity for the nobility and the priestly class. But Whitman turns this notion on its head. Rather than being a set of signs reserved for a hieratic or priestly class, the hieroglyphic of grass grows under everyone's feet as the uniform sign of human brotherhood. Whitman uses the commonest language, American slang, to name the various peoples: the Canadian Canuck, the Tuckahoe plantation owner, the "cuff" or old man, and the congressman. Speaking in the first person, the poet says that the hieroglyph of the grass "means [...] I give them the same, I receive them the same." The grass is thus a sign of the poet's regard for his fellow human beings, and of their essential equality with one another, regardless of race, class, region, or age.

Up to this point Whitman has defined the grass as meaning alternately the personal, the divine, the natural, and the social. These possible meanings are presented as if occurring to the poet one after the other, but none of them excludes the others, and none takes precedence. On the contrary, the multiple meanings of the grass are in keeping with its universality, like the book itself, *Leaves of Grass*, in which this poem is printed. The poet's final impression, however, subsumes those that have preceded it: "And now it seems to me the beautiful uncut hair of graves." The image is of both death and life. The grave is our common destination as human beings, but for Whitman death means neither finitude nor nothingness, much less the ascent to some heavenly realm. It means to be buried in the ground, there to nourish new life in forms that combine the human and the natural: the grass as "beautiful uncut hair." Rendered in this almost uncanny image, the meaning of the grass abolishes the difference between the human and the natural, and between life and death. But the grass never loses its simple and common quality. Whitman's poem shows how the mystery of creation resides even in the humblest parts of life and nature, in the things we see every day, under our feet. It is another kind of truth from that proposed by Pope. Pope's version of humility recognizes the truth of reason, unobstructed by pride, in passing judgment, including on one's own work. Whitman's humility is one of universal affirmation. It refuses judgment altogether, in homage to the truth that every living thing has its rightful place in the world.

Whitman's passionate engagement with the world, giving and receiving the same from everyone, stands in stark contrast to Emily Dickinson's instinct to keep clear of the world's attention. In the following poem, she has something to say about the perils of self-promotion, while humorously taking refuge in being "nobody":

> I'm Nobody! Who are you?
> Are you—Nobody—too?
> Then there's a pair of us!
> Don't tell! they'd advertise—you know!
>
> How dreary—to be—Somebody!
> How public—like a Frog—
> To tell one's name—the livelong June—
> To an admiring Bog!

The poem can be read as a justification for Dickinson's privacy and her dislike of publication, turning upside down the worldly value of being "somebody." While the status of being "nobody" is celebrated, she also finds companionship in another nobody, real or imagined. The last line of the first stanza is slightly odd, like many things in Dickinson. It says that if the obscurity of the two nobodies were to become known, then others would advertise it. But why? There is nothing noteworthy about being nobody; on the contrary, that is what being nobody means. What Dickinson suggests is that to be nobody is a privileged condition. It is freedom from the pressure to conform. Being advertised it would be ruined, as if a secret place of refuge were exposed. The inversion of conventional measures of importance continues in the second stanza with a satirical picture of what it means to be somebody. It takes a name to be somebody, and the frog literally makes a name for himself by telling it incessantly to an admiring public, here reduced to the nature of a bog to show what that admiration is worth. Dickinson's simplicity of language and lightness of tone are themselves marks of humility. In seeming not to take herself seriously, Dickinson has a serious point to make about the quality of humility.

A similar point is made by T.S. Eliot, with his characteristic solemnity and spiritual reflection, in "East Coker." East Coker is a village in Somerset from which Eliot's ancestors journeyed to America in the seventeenth century. He visited there in 1936 and 1937, entering the old stone chapel of St Michael and All Angels. He did not write about the place for three years, and eventually began his poem as a kind of exercise on the model of "Burnt Norton," written, like the earlier poem, in five sections of differing verse forms. However tentative its origins, "East Coker" was well received, and became the second of what were to be the *Four Quartets*. The poem begins with a statement of finitude, "In my beginning is my end," followed by images of the destruction of old houses like the ones in East Coker, and the mortality of human life as "Eating and drinking. Dung and death." It is a vision designed to inspire humility.

The second section is more contemplative. A rather strained evocation of the November landscape provokes the poet's own judgment of his effort as "not very satisfactory: A periphrastic study in a worn-out poetical fashion." The tone of humility is thus introduced as a caution against the temptation to make grand pronouncements, and leads to the startling confession, coming from a great poet, that "the poetry does not matter." Eliot at 52 is already a smiling public man of the kind who gives speeches at award dinners. In his letters and conversations with friends, he confesses his fear of having lost the creative energy that enabled him to write powerful and disruptive poems like *The Waste Land*. The war, in which Eliot had his part as an air raid warden, also made it difficult to gain the concentration needed to write poetry. His solution is to write precisely about the serenity he cannot obtain, and the humility needed for it. In this second section of "East Coker," he wonders what happened to the "Long hoped for calm, the autumnal serenity And the wisdom of age?"—and concludes that there is, "at best, only a limited value In the knowledge derived from experience." The problem is that this kind of knowledge falsifies experience by imposing a pattern upon it, whereas with every new moment the pattern has to be adjusted, "and every moment is a new and shocking Valuation of all we have been." Every moment is exceptional and has something unprecedented about it, necessarily altering our view of the experience we have lived up to that moment. Therefore, says the poet, the wisdom of old men is a myth. Rather,

> The only wisdom we can hope to acquire Is the wisdom of humility: humility is endless.

Everything in the poem up to this point has led to this conclusion. Houses rise and fall, human beings live and die. The poet's efforts are doomed to failure. The wisdom of old age is a fraud. Surely Eliot has in mind the preacher of Ecclesiastes, to whom "vanity of vanities, all is vanity" (Eccl. 1:2). If we cannot acquire wisdom through experience and age, "the only wisdom we can hope to acquire is that of humility." There is more than one reason why humility is endless. The first is the difficulty of attaining to it. In 1931, Eliot had written an essay on the *Pensées* of Pascal, for whom "discourses on humility are a source of pride in the vain," and Eliot himself had written in an essay on Shakespeare and Seneca, "Humility is the most difficult of all virtues to achieve; nothing dies harder than the desire to think well of oneself." In this sense, it is the effort to achieve an authentic humility that is an endless process.

Another reason for humility's endlessness is the one expressed in the 1618 Christmas Day sermon preached by Bishop Lancelot Andrewes in London. Among those in attendance was King James I, whose worldly eminence would have made the lesson on humility especially apposite. Eliot knew the sermon intimately. Andrewes's scriptural citation on this occasion was Luke 2:12: "And this shall be a sign unto you; ye shall find the Babe wrapped in swaddling clothes, lying in a manger." In his sermon, Andrewes points out that the coming of the Saviour is announced in the form of the greatest humility, intended for those of humble condition, "so that this is a sign for you, you who keep sheep, and such other poor people; you have a Saviour too." He adds that humility is a condition for anyone of whatever condition, to find Christ: "Humility then: we shall find Him by that sign, where we find humility, and not fail; and where that is not, be sure we shall never find Him." In Eliot's poem, the line on humility is followed by two lines which mark the destruction wrought by time—the disappearance of the houses, the death of the dancers—and the sense of absence which follows. This recognition of the ephemeral in human habitation and celebration prepares the soul for the humility necessary to its redemption. Humility is endless, then, as a condition for eternal salvation, and as the nature of salvation once achieved.

However, in the contemplative tradition of the *negative way* practiced by Christian figures such as the sixteenth-century John of the Cross, humility is not just a form of knowledge, but rather a form of ignorance. Eliot writes:

> In order to arrive at what you do not know
>   You must go by a way which is the way of ignorance.
> In order to possess what you do not possess
>   You must go by the way of dispossession.

Only through this evacuation of knowledge, possession, and desire—this creation of an inner clearing—does the soul prepare a place for the Holy Spirit to enter. The final section of the poem returns to the condition of old age, and confirms that far from bringing wisdom, "As we grow older The world becomes stranger." The poet's response to this is that "Old men ought to be explorers" always moving

> Into another intensity
> For a further union, a deeper communion
> Through the dark cold and empty desolation

With images of the vast waters of the sea, the poem concludes by inverting its opening line: The initial "In my beginning is my end" finally becomes "In my end is my beginning." Roethke's "The Far Field" would later show that this kind of spiritual movement is not limited to the Christian tradition. The contemplation of life's finitude and the endless return to humility ensuing from that contemplation are conditions for the awareness of infinity. Eliot's ashes are buried in the churchyard of St Michael and All Angels in East Coker. Under a window in the northwest corner of the sanctuary, a plaque bears the following inscription: "Of your charity pray for the repose of the soul of Thomas Stearns Eliot, poet [...] 'In my end is my beginning.' "

There are any number of reasons for a poet to exercise humility. While Pope ostensibly addresses the critic, he implies that poets as well need to know the truth of their own defects. He calls for a certain self-effacement before the work itself. For Eliot this self-effacement is a given, but he also claims that "the poetry does not matter," in the sense that one arrives at enlightenment from another kind of discipline, which poetry can only evoke indirectly. As for Dickinson, her diffidence concerns not poetry, "a fairer house than prose," but the poet's place in society. According to this view, one especially prevalent in modern poetry, neither the poet nor the poetry matters to the world. In Andrewes's Christmas sermon precisely this worldly insignificance was matter for inspiration, and so it is as well, in a secular context, for modern poets. A moving example is Dylan Thomas's "In My Craft or Sullen Art," first published in 1946. The title of the poem is evidence of Thomas's refusal to glorify his work, which is only a craft or at best a "sullen" art, the adjective implying estrangement from the world and from more exalted forms of artistic creation. Given this inauspicious premise, the poem seeks to justify a labor rewarded by neither fortune nor fame. It begins with an image of the poet working at night by the light of the moon, when "lovers lie abed With all their griefs in their arms." The poet then begins to name the things for which he is *not* working: neither ambition nor bread, nor the recognition that comes from charming the audiences at his readings, where Thomas, incidentally, cut a famously rakish and romantic figure. Rather than this, the poet of "In My Craft" writes—referring to the lovers abed—"for the common wages of their most secret heart." The full meaning of this is deferred for a few more lines, while the poet resumes his enumeration of those for whom he does not write: not for the proud man, nor for the dead,

> But for the lovers, their arms
> Round the griefs of the ages,
> Who pay no praise or wages
> Nor heed my craft or art.

Thomas says that he writes for the lovers "on these spindrift pages": spindrift is sea spray, like that which is visible from the cottage at New Quay in Cardigan Bay, where Thomas was living when he wrote this poem. The image suggests the ephemeral nature of these lines. They are written neither for the proud man nor for the towering dead of the poetic tradition, with their nightingales and psalms. The "raging moon," an image out of Yeats, stands as a symbol for the poet's lonely inspiration. His writing is for the lovers and the age-old emotion they embody, though they give him neither praise nor wages, nor even pay heed to his obscure "craft or art." In this designation he returns to the language of the first line, as if still not sure what to call his work. There is no doubt a measure of pride in the claim to work for no worldly reward, while the ambiguous name given to the poet's "craft or sullen art" is designed to fend off the notion that this is "art for art's sake." However, in its melancholy, singing phrases, the poem speaks of powerful feelings—of the sullenness, rage, grief, and love—shared by those who live and work in obscurity. The poet says, modestly enough, that his reward is to have spoken for them even if to them he remains unknown.

For a poet the sources of humility are not limited to the practice of poetry, to the marginalization it imposes, or even to the quest for a "deeper communion" beyond the domain of art. It can be profoundly personal, like a son's feeling for the sacrifices made for him by his father. This is the subject of Robert Hayden's "Those Winter Sundays," first published in 1966. The poem recalls the poet's childhood in a poor neighborhood of Detroit, where he was raised by foster parents. The opening lines describe how the man he called his father got up early on "Sundays, too" in the depth of winter in order to light fires to warm the house. Setting about his chores stoically in the "blueblack cold" before dawn, he made the fires with hands cracked and aching from his weekday labor. He polished his son's good shoes. "No one ever thanked him." The poem concludes with the rueful retrospection of the adult poet:

> What did I know, what did I know
> of love's austere and lonely offices?

The work has been done while the child sleeps, so that he awakens to the sound of the splintering fire already warming the house, and waits for his father's call before rising and dressing. The "chronic angers" of the family have made the child fearful and distant, as the adult poet now recalls. The poet's foster father, William Hayden, was a devout Baptist who held his family to high standards of rectitude, and often quarreled with his wife. Only now does the poet acknowledge, in retrospect, the injustice of his childish indifference toward the man who, out of love, had driven out the cold and polished his child's shoes in preparation for church.

The tone of regret, introduced in the first stanza with the observation that no one ever thanked his father, is redoubled in the final lines, with the repeated question: "what did I know of love's austere and lonely offices?" William Hayden died many years before this poem was written, so that Robert Hayden said of this poem in an interview, "What hurts me is that he never lived to know that I cared that much." The austere and lonely offices are now those of the poet as well, with his perfect iambic rhythms, his tone of disciplined restraint, and his humility toward the memory of his father, a day laborer who knew nothing of poetry but knew how to raise a son. As a purely rhetorical question, the answer to the poem's final question is "nothing." But the poet knew enough as a child to remember, perhaps 40 years later, the cracked skin of his father's hands, the sensations of waking in that house, and even the polish his father put on his good shoes. What the mature poet adds to these sensations is the knowledge of love, of the sacrifice it demands, and the humility it teaches. However personal the feelings recorded here, the circumstances that inspire them are rendered in objective detail, and the poem's conclusion gives them universal meaning.

This chapter began with the proposition that a condition for humility is the knowledge that one matters to others insofar as one finds meaningful forms of relation with them. The idea of humility as human relation has been affirmed, though in very different ways, by several of the poems surveyed here. Pope advises the writer to "trust not yourself," but to rely on others to point out your defects. Whitman's image of the common grass is made the symbol of his disposition for a universal fellowship with men and woman of all conditions. Dickinson, though "nobody," seeks a companion in obscurity: "there's a pair of us!" Thomas writes for lovers, and by implication for all human beings of a passionate nature, however indifferent they may be to his work. Hayden's praise of his father, acknowledging his own childish ignorance and indifference, is a poignant exercise in humility. Only Eliot, in his negative way through ignorance and dispossession, does not openly seek human relation. Instead, he seeks "a further union, a deeper communion" which we are left to interpret in metaphysical terms. As we have seen, however, this communion depends on a conscious emptying-out of faith, hope, and love, a movement which constitutes its own kind of humility. In this cultivation of nothingness, Eliot has a rival in his contemporary, Wallace Stevens.

Stevens's first book of poems, *Harmonium* (1923), explores the idea of a world without God, where human beings are "unsponsored" and free of heavenly influence in their relations with one another and with nature. Thousands of years of religious faith have made this state of affairs difficult for the modern mind to grasp, so that we are constantly tempted to invent substitutes for the loss of God: the spirit of nature, the transcendence of the soul, the redeeming power of art, and so on. Only the most honest and rigorous mind is able to gaze upon the world without investing it with these illusions. Such is the subject of Stevens's poem, "The Snow Man." The snow man is the one capable of looking at the various evergreens laden with snow and ice, capable of hearing the sound of the wind over the bare land—without thinking of any misery in the winter scene, because misery belongs only to human beings. Rather, such a man is the listener, who, "nothing himself, beholds Nothing that is not there and the nothing that is." What the snow man represents is pure clarity of perception, free of human constructs like "beauty" and "meaning."

The poem's opening lines introduce a kind of ideal person contemplating a winter landscape with a "mind of winter." The word "landscape" is not used, however, as that would burden the scene with received notions of what it should look like. Instead, the poem evokes distinct objects in sharply visual detail: "the boughs Of the pine-trees crusted with snow," "the junipers shagged with ice." The austerity of vision called for does not prevent the scene from being described with dazzling beauty, as in "The spruces rough in the distant glitter Of the January sun." Stevens's point is that only the mind of winter, conditioned by a body that has been cold a long time, is capable of beholding such a scene without falsely endowing it with aesthetic, spiritual, or moral value. The mind of winter, then, has a cold purity untouched by the chimeras of myth. It does not project human feeling onto objects in nature, and so does not think there is misery in the sound of the wind or of a few leaves scattered by the wind. The mind beholding the scene has become the listener, with the same freedom from illusion in what he hears as in what he sees. What he hears is merely the sound of the land full of the wind "blowing in the same bare place." Stevens is careful to avoid the language of the Romantics, for whom, in Wordsworth's phrase, "love of nature lead[s] to love of man." There is no love in Stevens's scene, but there is a shared vacancy of man and nature, for the snow man who sees and listens with such clarity, nothing in himself, beholds "Nothing that is not there and the nothing that is."

There is thus a difference between Stevens and Eliot. Eliot seeks in the dark night of the soul a darkness "which shall be the darkness of God"; he counsels himself to wait without thought "for you are not ready for thought." The end of this waiting is nothing less than revelation, so that "the darkness shall be the light, and the stillness the dancing." In direct contrast to this, the revelation in Stevens is precisely the absence of revelation, or the revelation of absence. The nothing that is there at the conclusion of his poem is the bare land, divested of the enchantments devised by the imagination. The rigorous application of this vision requires that the snow man himself behold his own nothingness, when emptied of the products of that same imagination. To behold this nothingness is an exercise in absolute humility, beyond even that of Eliot. Does Stevens therefore refuse the power of imagination? On the contrary, he insists that we exist as human beings by virtue of that power, through our capacity to imagine ourselves in the various and extravagant ways in which we have always done so. For Stevens the most powerful instrument of imagination is language, for it is in language that we define ourselves and our world. If imagination works through language, then poetry as the highest form of language must be the supreme manifestation of imagination, or as Stevens puts it, the supreme fiction. Only we must have the humility to recognize it as a fiction, founded on the void of nothingness. There need be nothing shocking in this, for Stevens is saying merely that our world is what we have made it, and that we are what we have made ourselves. When we behold our unhappy world and our imperfect selves in this light, it is hard to avoid feelings of humility. But then again, if from nothing we have made ourselves and the world, this also means that we and the world are what we make it.

Why be on the side of humility in a world that encourages self-promotion? Poets have given us reasons. Pope tells us that humility allows us to know truth, and betters our judgment. Whitman shows, in the image of the grass, how humility breaks down the boundaries we have erected against one another, and makes us all equal. We all walk on the same earth, under the same sky. Dickinson's "nobody" lives happily in retreat from the "admiring bog" of the public. Eliot's humility clears a space in his soul for the Holy Spirit to dwell. Stevens makes that same vacancy for the work of human imagination. In doing so, he implies that humility is closer to hope than to despair.

Note

1 Levinas, *Totalité et infinité*. Paris: Livre de poche, 1987, p. 196. My translation.

Discovery

Let me begin with an old story of discovery, told in the gospel of Luke. On the day after Jesus died, two of his disciples were joined by the resurrected Christ on the road from Jerusalem to Emmaus, but failed to recognize him: "Their eyes were holden that they should not know him" (24:16). At the end of the day, when they were at table, Jesus took bread, and blessed, and broke it, and gave it to them. At this moment, "their eyes were opened, and they knew him; and he vanished out of their sight" (24:31). The story has a near parallel in John. Earlier on the same day Mary Magdalene, weeping at Jesus's tomb, turned around to see him standing there, "but knew not that it was Jesus" (20:14). Supposing him to be the gardener, she asked where the body of Jesus lay. "Jesus saith unto her, Mary. She turned herself, and saith unto him, Rabboni; which is to say, Master" (20:16). For Jesus to call Mary by her name means that she is known to him, and in the same moment she knows him as well. The simple exchange of names is more moving than any other speech could be, for everything takes place in what is unsaid: Christ is risen. Taken together, the two stories have elements in common which can tell us something about the nature of discovery. Both of them involve a journey or an actual search. Both are examples of misrecognition, in which the witnesses fail to see what is before their eyes. Then comes the sudden revelation, when their eyes are opened. In both cases, the discovery of Jesus resurrected is the object of wonder, of something improbable and unforeseen, and the cause of joy. And in both cases this discovery profoundly changes those who behold him.

In what follows I want to show how poetry, like scripture, conveys the experience of discovery in ways that reflect poetry's fundamental quality of disclosure, of opening our eyes to the world in such a way that we see it anew, and are changed by doing so. The sudden revelation in the Gospel story constitutes the mode of discovery in which something radically new is revealed to the beholder. The journey to Emmaus is symbolic of the wandering or exploration that leads to discovery, and the moment when the disciples' eyes were opened corresponds to the nature of discovery as the ability to see what is before us as it really is. These three elements—revelation, exploration, vision—offer a way to organize our reading of a series of poems of discovery.

Discovery as revelation: The object of discovery may be something less exalted than the resurrection of Christ. One of the most famous sonnets in English is about the discovery of a book. In 1816, John Keats was a young intern at Guy's Hospital in London, but he increasingly felt his true vocation to be poetry. One evening in October, his former schoolmaster,

Charles Cowden Clarke, invited him to see a 200 year-old edition of George Chapman's translation of Homer, the first in English. Keats and Clarke pored over the volume until six in the morning, when Keats left Clarke's cottage in Hampstead, north of London, to return to his own lodgings on the South Bank. Keats began composing his sonnet on the way home, finished it before leaving for work, and sent it off to Clarke:

> Much have I travell'd in the realms of gold,
> And many goodly states and kingdoms seen;
> Round many western islands have I been
> Which bards in fealty to Apollo hold.
> Oft of one wide expanse had I been told
> That deep-brow'd Homer ruled as his demesne;
> Yet did I never breathe its pure serene
> Till I heard Chapman speak out loud and bold:
> Then felt I like some watcher of the skies
> When a new planet swims into his ken;
> Or like stout Cortez when with eagle eyes
> He star'd at the Pacific—and all his men
> Look'd at each other with a wild surmise—
> Silent, upon a peak in Darien.

At the age of 21, Keats's travels had been limited to the journey between London and the nearby village of Enfield. But his reading had taken him through many lands and ages past. The islands held by bards in loyalty to Apollo, god of the arts, are a figure for the literary works that have most marked the young poet. There was one "wide expanse," however, of which the poet had often heard as being the domain of Homer: the *Iliad* and *Odyssey*, until now closed to the young poet who did not read Greek. In imagining Homer's face as "deep-browed," Keats could have in mind Homer's imaginary portrait bust in the British Museum, or an engraving of his bust in the Louvre, both of which bear the blind poet's deep brows of wisdom and divine inspiration. Keats had indeed read Pope's early eighteenth-century translation of Homer, but thought it marred by the artificiality of its poetic diction. The purity and serenity of Homer's work could be revealed to Keats only by the "loud and bold" voice of the Elizabethan poet, Chapman.

At this point the sonnet turns from the initial octave, the eight lines that culminate in the discovery, to the sestet, the six lines that describe the effects of the discovery on the poet's imagination. Keats offers two analogies drawn from his early readings at school. The first is an account of William Herschel's discovery of the planet Uranus in 1781. The poet likens himself to the astronomer, "watcher of the skies," to whom the appearance of Chapman's translation is the equivalent of the new planet. The skies in their infinite expanse strewn with stars form a heavenly counterpart to the wide expanse of the Aegean studded with islands. It is also noteworthy, for a medical student torn between science and poetry, that the personal discovery of a poetical work should feel as momentous as one of the most important scientific discoveries of the day.

The other analogy is that of the discovery of the Pacific Ocean in 1513 by Vasco Nuñez de Balboa, here mistaken for the explorer Hernando Cortéz. In these final lines, Keats returns to his initial imagery of the sea. He evidently has in mind a passage in William Robertson's 1777 *History of America*, where Balboa and his men have crossed the isthmus of Panama from the Caribbean shore to a mountain in the southern region of Darien. Robertson writes that when Balboa and his men had climbed most of the mountain, Balboa commanded the others to halt, so that he could reach the summit alone:

> As soon as he beheld the South Sea [the Pacific], stretching in endless prospect below him, he fell on his knees, and lifting up his hands to Heaven, returned thanks to God, who had conducted him to a discovery so beneficial to his country, and so honourable to himself. His followers, observing his transports of joy, rushed forward to join in his wonder, exultation, and gratitude.

Keats's version of the same moment is perhaps historically mistaken but poetically more sublime, transforming the demonstrative celebration described in Robertson to a moment of silent wonder characterized as "wild surmise." The *Oxford English Dictionary* defines "surmise" as "an idea formed in the mind that something may be true, but without certainty and on very slight evidence." As used by Keats, the word aptly calls forth the state of mind of one who, having made a startling discovery, is so dazzled as to hardly know what to make of it. The analogy amounts to a great claim for poetry, for it makes the discovery of a poetical work as important as the discovery of an ocean. Both events open onto the infinite. In any case, for Keats this moment is the culmination of several stages: the journey on foot across London to behold the antique volume, the revelation of Homer's world through the clear voice of Chapman, the immediate and lasting effect on Keats himself. But discoveries like this are rarely made by chance. Herschel has been a watcher of the skies, Balboa an intrepid explorer. Keats, as his opening lines tell us, has been an explorer in his own right, and has prepared all his young life for the encounter with Chapman. The readiness is all.

Keats's discovery is exceptional in that it reveals something rare and previously unknown to him. But a poet like Wordsworth can make something revelatory out of an everyday discovery, as when on a country ramble he comes suddenly on a field of daffodils. His poem on this subject was written in April 1804, when the poet was living at Dove Cottage, Grasmere, in the lake district of Westmoreland. His sister Dorothy recorded the event in her journal for April 15. She and William were out walking by Ullswater Lake when they came on the yellow flowers, which became more and more abundant as they approached, finally appearing as "a long belt of them along the shore, about the breadth of a country turnpike road." A breeze gives motion to the daffodils, as Dorothy writes: "they tossed and reeled and danced, and seemed as if they verily laughed with the wind [...]; they looked so gay, ever glancing, ever changing."

William's poem has much the same imagery, as if brother and sister had shared their impressions on the spot. But the poet renders the discovery as a solitary experience. He begins:

> I wandered lonely as a cloud
> That floats on high o'er vales and hills,
> When all at once I saw a crowd,
> A host, of golden daffodils;
> Beside the lake, beneath the trees,
> Fluttering and dancing in the breeze.

We know from Dorothy that the poet was not alone, but the loneliness will be justified for poetic reasons. The image of wandering like a cloud is borrowed from Wordsworth's *The Prelude* (of which more later), but here the lonely wanderer is a figure of melancholy, in stark contrast to the host of golden flowers dancing gaily in the breeze. Wandering itself is a prelude to discovery, so that to come upon the daffodils "all at once" is to make a lasting impression on the poet's sensibility.

The next two stanzas of the poem compare the profusion of daffodils to the stars in the Milky Way. The waves of the lake beside them dance, but the flowers outdo them in their glee. The vision is one of boundless joy in a natural form that stretches "in never-ending line Along the margin of a bay." The real point of the poem, however, is the effect of the discovery on the poet. At first, he is merely delighted by the scene without understanding what it means. He redoubles his gaze in what is no more than a kind of dazed wonder:

> A poet could not but be gay,
> In such a jocund company:
> I gazed—and gazed—but little thought
> What wealth the show to me had brought.

To call the scene a "show" implies not just that the poet has witnessed a performance in the dance of the daffodils, but also that a hidden enchantment in nature has been revealed to him, as if in a forest clearing he had come upon a dance of fairies. It is left for the final lines to assess the enduring value of the show:

> For oft, when on my couch I lie
> In vacant or in pensive mood,
> They flash upon that inward eye
> Which is the bliss of solitude;

> And then my heart with pleasure fills,
> And dances with the daffodils.

In poetry, the importance of a discovery is not in how it changes our knowledge of the heavens or the seas, but in the way one feels, in how it transforms the poet, and possibly us as readers. The concluding lines of Wordsworth's poem thus make a temporal shift from the anecdote of a remembered incident to a recurring experience in the poet's present life. The idle poet on the couch contrasts with the active wanderer, but the vacant or pensive mood is the same: he relives the moment of delight each time as if it were the first: the daffodils "flash upon that inward eye Which is the bliss of solitude." The "wealth" of this discovery is that the loneliness of the wanderer has been transformed by memory, and by poetic re-creation, into the bliss of solitude.

Samuel Taylor Coleridge, who considered Wordsworth the greatest of living poets, nonetheless found fault with this poem. He thought the inward eye and bliss of solitude should be reserved for something more profound than the memory of a mere visual impression. He objected as well to the banality of the final couplet, to which "we seem to sink most abruptly, not to say burlesquely" from what goes before. Let us grant the justice of these remarks. But the virtue of Wordsworth's poem is in what we might call its transferable value. Any reader can share in the experience it conveys of discovery and of simple pleasure in recollection.

It may not be every reader who can share the experience of catching a fish that turns into a girl. Such is the discovery made in Yeats's poem "The Song of Wandering Aengus," which nonetheless has an allegorical meaning relevant even to the lives of those who are unaccustomed to supernatural occurrences. As a young poet, William Butler Yeats considered his vocation to be the revival of certain legends that survived mainly in the oral traditions of the Gaelic-speaking west of Ireland. This poem is spoken by the figure of Aengus, a god associated in Irish mythology with love and lovers:

> I went out to the hazel wood,
> Because a fire was in my head,
> And cut and peeled a hazel wand,
> And hooked a berry to a thread;
> And when white moths were on the wing,
> And moth-like stars were flickering out,
> I dropped the berry in a stream
> And caught a little silver trout.
>
> When I had laid it on the floor
> I went to blow the fire a-flame,
> But something rustled on the floor,
> And someone called me by my name:
> It had become a glimmering girl
> With apple blossom in her hair

> Who called me by my name and ran
> And faded through the brightening air.
>
> Though I am old with wandering
> Through hollow lands and hilly lands,
> I will find out where she has gone,
> And kiss her lips and take her hands;
> And walk among long dappled grass,
> And pluck till time and times are done,
> The silver apples of the moon,
> The golden apples of the sun.

In the first part of the poem, Aengus is seized by a passion or inspiration—"a fire was in my head"—which leads him to fashion a fishing rod out of the elements of nature most near at hand, a hazel wand and a berry. The time is the hour just before dawn, when the stars are flickering out. He catches a little silver trout, which he lays on the floor beside the fire as if to prepare it for cooking. But then, in the second stanza, something marvelous occurs. He hears his name called, and discovers that the silver trout has become a "glimmering girl." Again she calls his name, before fading in the brightening air of the new day. According to folkloric tradition, the fairies who come out at night must disappear with the light of dawn. Thus in Shakespeare's *Midsummer Night's Dream*, Puck warns the fairy king, Oberon, that he hears the morning lark, and Oberon must disappear with Titania into the night: "Then, my queen, in silence sad, Trip we after the night's shade" (IV:1). In the final stanza of Yeats's poem, we learn that the story of the glimmering girl is from Aengus's youth, on which he now reflects as an old man. Since that moment by the stream he has wandered his whole life in search of the girl. He has been transformed from a fisherman to a wanderer who dreams of finding the girl, loving her, and spending the rest of time with her in an enchanted world, plucking "the silver apples of the moon, The golden apples of the sun."

These images are based on the original discovery: the silver apples recall the silver trout from which the girl was transformed, as well as the apple blossom in her hair. The golden apples of the sun recall the brightening air through which she has disappeared. To pluck the apples of both colors adds to the sense of plenitude and harmony. The dream is to unite the worlds of night and day, of nature and the supernatural, as well as the poet's age and his youth. In a note to this poem, Yeats identifies its source as a Gaelic poem of the previous century whose images are of "the desire of the man 'which is for the woman,' and the 'the desire of the woman which is for the desire of the man,' and of all desires that are as these."

The poem begins with Aengus's desire in the form of a "fire" in his head. When the girl appears magically before him, it is not so much his discovery as she who "discovers" herself to him as a revelation, something new and strange which sets him wandering forever after in the hope of rediscovering her. The terms of the Gaelic poem are thus obliquely fulfilled: he desires her, whereas she has obtained his desire for her. If we consider the perpetual nature of Aengus's desire in itself, the poem is a parable not just of revelation but of the eternal desire for a new life based on the recovery of a lost innocence. To the extent that such a recovery is impossible, the poem is imbued with a wistful melancholy. Having grown old with wandering, Aengus will wander still, having discovered, nonetheless, the object of his life.

Discovery as exploration. Discovery may be the consequence of the search for a given goal, such as an ocean, or the poet may come upon it in the course of a journey without a given object, as Keats seems to have done in the course of his varied but unschooled reading. Discovery comes to the wanderer as well as to the deliberate searcher. This is one of the lessons of Wordsworth's epic autobiographical poem, the first of its kind in English, *The Prelude*. The poem begins with the poet having left the city at age 29, and finding himself free to "fix my habitation where I will":

> The earth is all before me: with a heart
> Joyous, nor scared of its own liberty,
> I look about, and should the guide I choose
> Be nothing better than a wandering cloud,
> I cannot miss my way.

Wordsworth has in mind the conclusion of Milton's *Paradise Lost*, where Adam and Eve, having been expelled from Eden, must now make their way through the world:

> The world was all before them, where to choose
> Their place of rest, and Providence their guide.
>
> XII: 646–647

Wordsworth thus begins where that other great English epic has ended, while taking Milton's story in a new direction. Rather than being expelled from Eden, the poet of Wordsworth's poem is freed from the prison of the city to wander happily where he will, with his heart as his only guide. He cannot miss his way because he has no way other than that of freedom. The lonely wanderer who discovers a field of daffodils is one version of this poetic figure.

Wordsworth's claim that the wanderer unafraid of his own liberty cannot lose his way is shared by Whitman, for whom the *Song of the Open Road* serves as a kind of manifesto of the wandering spirit. Whitman begins in a way that echoes *The Prelude*, itself an echo of *Paradise Lost*:

> Afoot and light-hearted I take to the open road,
> Healthy, free, the world before me,
> The long brown path before me leading wherever I choose.

Whitman appropriates a theme in English poetry and adapts it to the American landscape, pursuing it further than any poet has done before. In Milton, Adam and Eve find the world all before them only at the conclusion of that great epic. In Wordsworth, the poet's sense of release is more literary than biographical: with the earth all before him, he retires to his cottage in Grasmere in order to write about his past.

Whitman's poem, by contrast, takes place in an evolving present which constantly moves into the future. It inaugurates an American art form of nomadic exploration whose manifestations are as far-reaching as Jack Kerouac's novel *On the Road* (1957) and Dennis Hopper's 1969 film *Easy Rider*. The poet of *Song of the Open Road* asks not for good fortune, for "I am myself good fortune." The long brown path he follows is that of the earth; he needs neither the constellations to navigate his way, nor any hope of heaven, for "the earth, that is sufficient." What Whitman hopes to discover is no less than everything to be encountered on the road, including much that is unseen—invisible, and to be discovered only through experience. This experience includes what he calls "the profound lesson of reception," by which he will extend an accepting hand to those on whom society turns its back: "the black with his woolly head, the felon, the diseas'd, the illiterate person, are not denied." Yet more than this, the poet calls out to the very air and light of the road, to the objects that give shape to his meanings, and says to them, "I believe you are latent with unseen existences." The unseen for Whitman is both that which is yet to be seen in his wanderings, and that which lies hidden behind appearances—the secret existence of things of which he seeks revealment: "From all that has touch'd you I believe you have imparted to yourselves, and now would impart secretly to me." The kind of discovery the poet seeks, however, is not one that creates amazement or astonishment. Neither "a thousand perfect men" nor "a thousand beautiful forms of women" would astonish or amaze him. Rather, what he seeks is wisdom:

> Wisdom is of the soul, is not susceptible of proof, is its own proof,
> Applies to all stages and objects and qualities and is content,
> Is the certainty of the reality and immortality of things, and the excellence of things,
> Something there is in the float and the sight of things that provokes it out of the soul.

This wisdom comes from the discovery that "Here is realization," that the world is fully realized to the soul ready to receive it and reach out to it. "Efflux" is Whitman's word for the force that flows from the soul:

> The efflux of the soul is happiness, here is happiness,
> I think it pervades the open air, waiting at all times,
> Now it flows into us, we are rightly charged.

The soul seems to be something between the poet and the world which pervades both, and which gives rise to the "fluid and attaching character" which is "the freshness and sweetness of man and woman." In other words, it is love in the universal sense, which binds human beings to one another and to the world of objects and nature around them. Whitman suggests, however, that there is an eternal movement to this fluid and attaching character which calls for the poet to travel tirelessly on the open road:

> Allons! whoever you are come travel with me!
> Traveling with me you find what never tires.

The finding of what never tires is not a single happenstance that constitutes its own end, like Keats's looking into Chapman's *Homer* or Wordsworth's sight of a host of daffodils. Rather, for Whitman it is a way of life, the never-ending process of discovering the world and one's relation to it. This means that the traveler on the open road must never stop, however sweet the inducement of possessions, of home, of hospitality. Such things are indeed to be cherished, but "we are permitted to receive [them] but a little while," and then they must be kept only in memory, like Wordsworth's flowers. Eliot writes that old men ought to be explorers, but in Whitman this imperative extends to persons of every age and condition. The danger lies in satisfaction, in quiescence and stagnation. We must not rest content with what we know. "We cannot remain here." Whitman therefore urges us on:

> Allons! the inducements shall be greater,
> We will sail pathless and wild seas,
> We will go where winds blow, waves dash, and the Yankee clipper
>   speeds by under full sail.

The poem ends with an appeal to the reader which may recall Jesus's repeated calls to his disciples to "follow me," as in Matthew 4:19: "Follow me, and I will make you fishers of men." But Whitman is not the Christ; he speaks simply of the love of human beings for one another on this earth, an ideal which demands that he give himself as much to his fellow traveler as that person gives to him:

> Camerado, I give you my hand!
> I give you my love more precious than money,
> I give you myself before preaching or law;
> Will you give me yourself? will you come travel with me?
> Shall we stick by each other as long as we live?

It is the offer of comradeship, not of discipleship; it is to "travel with me" rather than to follow me; it is made not by a divine being but by one mortal to another, and not for eternity but for "as long as we live."

And yet there is something deeply religious in Whitman's devotion to his fellow beings, at least in the original sense of *religio*, a connection between people, a bond. Throughout the poem as a whole, Whitman offers his own sense of discovery both as readiness and acceptance: a readiness to accept that which is already realized, to see and know it for what it is. The implication is that discovery is a question of opening our eyes. Like Mary Magdalene facing the risen Christ, we fail to recognize what is before us because it does not conform to our notions of how the world or other human beings should be. We have not yet learned "the lesson of reception," which would allow us to receive without prejudice the felon, the stranger, and the ignorant, and to discover the humanity that each possesses no less than ourselves. In Whitman's poem this discovery is not of a fact or of a known object. It is rather a demeanor, a disposition to see the world not through a glass darkly, but face to face.

Discovery as vision. There is a kind of discovery that depends not on the sudden appearance of something completely new, nor on a course of exploration or even aimless wandering. It rather depends on what the French call *l'oeil éveillé*, the awakened eye capable of seeing even ordinary objects as if for the first time. Part of this renewed vision of things lies in beholding "nothing that is not there," like Stevens's Snow Man, suggesting that ideas about things are what prevent us from seeing things as they are. If only we could get past those ideas, we might discover—not the truth, for the truth is another idea—but what we might call the real. This is the subject of Stevens's "The Latest Freed Man." This man is "Tired of the old descriptions of the world." The poem begins with this line, then shows the man rising at six, sitting on the edge of his bed, and looking out at the landscape. The man speaks to himself, saying, "I suppose there is A doctrine to this landscape." Yet, what he sees is the color and mist of the morning, and the rain, the sea, and the sun of the moment. This perception is enough for him. The effort is to see the landscape independently of doctrine or of truth as an abstraction. To discover it as it is in the moment is sufficient to overcome the doctrine: it is enough. One is reminded of certain painters, like Cézanne, whom Stevens admired, and who consciously sought to render the landscape in a manner free of classical values. The strong man presented here is Stevens's figure for the man free of doctrine, who is transformed, just for that moment on rising, "from a doctor into an ox." The doctor is the man who brings knowledge and doctrine to what he sees; the ox signifies strength without doctrine, and the freedom of vision which comes with strength:

> It was everything bulging and blazing and big in itself,
> The blue of the rug, the portrait of Vidal,
> *Qui fait fi des joliesses banales*, the chairs.

Stevens faces the task of rendering the look of things without resorting to "description," the organization of the world in a heavily coded language. To do so, however difficult it may be, is to gain the freedom that the poet seeks, if we can compare the freed man to the poet himself. The claim is not for the importance of what things are, the oak-leaves, for example, but for the way they look. The way they look is real to the poet, and when freed of doctrine and description these things become more vivid, "everything bulging and blazing and big in itself"—an alliteration of "b"s that reproduces in the sound of words the heightened buzz of the moment. The concluding lines of the poem (above) enumerate those things, however banal in themselves: the blue of the rug, the chairs, the portrait of Anatole Vidal, the Parisian book dealer of whom Stevens possessed a portrait. Vidal is one who "couldn't care less for banal little prettinesses," an attitude Stevens shares. *Les joliesses banales* belong to the doctrine which causes us to see a landscape as "pretty as a postcard," and thus not really to see it freely, to discover how it really looks. To free oneself from such clichés requires strength of imagination. We need that strength to discover things for ourselves and so to make them more real.

This is exactly what Elizabeth Bishop does in a poem about catching a fish. We have seen Yeats's story of the silver trout that becomes a glimmering girl, but the stories of miraculous catches go back to the Bible, as in Luke's account of Jesus at the lake of Gennesaret. In that story, the fishermen have been toiling all night with nothing to show for it. But then Jesus enters one of the boats, urging them to cast their nets once more. They do so, not without hesitation, and bring in a catch so huge that it breaks their net. A miracle has taken place. They recognize Jesus as their Lord, "and when they had brought their ships to the land, they forsook all, and followed him" (Luke 5:11). The discovery here is not so much that of the fish as the power and benevolence of Jesus. In any case, it completely transforms the lives of the fishermen. They will follow their Lord for the rest of their lives, just as the wandering Aengus spends his life in pursuit of his more ephemeral vision. Bishop's own fish story unveils a number of discoveries, but they depend on neither supernatural nor divine intervention. Instead, she sees the richness and beauty of what is often overlooked in the most commonplace of things.

Her poem is written as a little story, in complete sentences that could be mistaken for vibrant prose if not for the line-breaks that call attention to each image in turn. It begins with the poet catching a tremendous fish which she holds half out of the water beside her boat. It is an old fish, "battered and venerable." Bishop's language itself is homely in its simplicity, with a kind of heft in the brevity and repetition of its lines that conveys the weight of the fish almost physically. However, a number of elements quickly establish something like intimacy between the poet and her fish: her hook fast in the fish's mouth, her wonder that he hadn't fought, her observation that this big old fish has a battered and venerable past. Following this simple introduction, the poet then looks more closely at the body of the fish: his brown skin hanging and patterned "like ancient wallpaper," his burden of barnacles and white sea-lice, and of "rags of green weed." This growing awareness of the fish—its body, shape, color, with the presence of other creatures clinging to it—is the first discovery of the poem. It consists of simply looking closely and being intensely aware of what is before her eyes. The poet indeed looks into the fish's eyes, which are shallow and yellow, with irises "backed and packed with tarnished tinfoil," but the fish doesn't look back. His eyes shift a little, not to return her stare, but more like "the tipping of an object toward the light." Bishop wavers between humanizing the fish, battle-scarred, sullen-faced—and acknowledging him as something completely other than she, an object in the light.

But then she makes a new discovery: from the fish's lower lip hang five old hooks, each attached to the remnants of lines broken when the fish got away. The lines hang in different colors and textures, "like medals with their ribbons frayed and wavering." Each is a trophy from a battle won, furthering the sense of the creature's weary knowledge, like that of an old, wounded admiral. They tell of a long history.

The poem's final discovery comes as a direct effect of the poet's intensifying stare. As, transfixed, she gazes at the fish, "victory filled up the little rented boat." The pool of oil in the bilge water spreads a rainbow around the rusted engine, the orange bailer, the old thwarts, oarlocks, and gunnels,

> —until everything
> was rainbow, rainbow, rainbow!
> And I let the fish go.

The victory in the first sense is of course the poet's victorious feeling in the moment. She has caught the fish that nobody else could catch. But there is another victory as well, one that justifies the rapture of the next few lines. The poet has discovered, in another species, signs of the relentless struggle for survival that unites all living creatures. The shadow of death in which this struggle takes place—be it the escape from predators, the pursuit of love, or the writing of poetry—is what lends beauty to life. That beauty manifests itself in the poem as a rainbow composed of the most unlikely elements: the oil in the bilge water, the rusted engine and bailer, the sun-cracked thwarts—homely objects with their own striking colors, like those of the fish. The word "rainbow" is said three times, as if the word itself, even repeated, were not enough to capture the experience of epiphany. In the Book of Genesis, the rainbow is the sign of God's covenant, of peace between man and God after the flood. Bishop's poem inherits some of the symbolic authority of that image, while adapting it to her own unassuming world. Her epiphany is the richness of life itself manifested in the old fish, the rented boat, the rusted bailer, and in her own capacity to discover beauty in these things. But this epiphany, however secular, echoes Noah's in its meaning of peace and promise for the creatures of the earth.

Bishop wrote this poem in 1940 when she was living in Key West, Florida, where she liked to go out fishing in the sea. She sent the poem to her friend Marianne Moore with the words, "I am sending you a real 'trifle.' I'm afraid it is very bad and, if not like Robert Frost, perhaps like Ernest Hemingway! I left the last line on it so it wouldn't be, I don't know..." Bishop could be thinking of Frost's poem "Two Look at Two," in which a pair of walkers in the woods come suddenly upon a pair of deer, and the two pairs stare at one another in a spellbound moment, "a great wave from it going over them." Her poem can be compared to Hemingway for the infinite care he takes in describing the catching and cooking of fish, for example, in his story "Big Two-Hearted River." But neither Frost nor Hemingway achieves, in these works, Bishop's sudden transformation of lowly objects into the substance of transcendence. In her letter to Moore, she is understandably doubtful of the final line, which lacks the poetic resonance of what precedes it. But the spell has to be broken somehow, and there is justice in giving the old fish one more chance to live. She has discovered that as well.

The forms of discovery witnessed in all of these poems are those of revealment, exploration, and intensified modes of seeing, but each poem has elements of all three. What is discovered in each case is cause for joy, and the poems show us that joy can be found in many things: in a book, in a flower, in the freedom of the road or the freedom from doctrine, even in an old fish. In his autobiographical work *Surprised by Joy*, C.S. Lewis writes that his greatest discovery was that what he calls Joy was not a state of mind or of body, but a kind of desire for something outside of the self, "for that unity which we can never reach except by ceasing to be the separate phenomenal beings we call 'we'." This discovery he experienced as a new freedom, a loosening of the reins that had held him within the confines of the self. He describes the journey of his soul as having gone from a philosophical idea of the Absolute to the Hegelian idea of Spirit, and finally to a Christian faith in God. Each of these steps was toward something more concrete, more immanent, and more compelling. In telling this story, Lewis offers us a framework for understanding the poems of discovery treated in this chapter. Each of them gives testimony to a moment of discovery that finds joy in something other than and outside of the self: "something there is in the float and the sight of things that provokes it out of the soul." Each of them makes the object of that desire into something concrete. What leads to discovery—in science, in love, in poetry—is this desire for a more perfect union with what is beyond us: a great poem, the morning's color and mist, divine being.

Parting

The parting of two persons who love each other is a form of loss. In Freud's 1917 essay "Mourning and Melancholia," he writes that the loss of a loved one is a cause of mourning, which itself involves several stages: incomprehension, the loss of interest in the outside world, the inability to adopt a new object of love. An increasing awareness of reality makes the mourner realize that the loved one is gone for good, and compels the mourner's desire to withdraw from its object, though not without resistance. Nonetheless, says Freud, "Normally, respect for reality gains the day." In the case of art, the process of loss and mourning takes on an independent being in the form of the art work; the poem in particular can transform suffering into an object of contemplation. In this process, one can be freed from suffering in some measure.

In what follows I wish to examine a number of ways in which poets have done something of this nature. Writing a poem may be therapeutic, but more important is that the poem speaks of the experience of parting in a new and distinct way, articulating it in new language. The poem is thus evidence of the uniqueness of every experience, and of the fundamental inexpressibility of loss. No poem can capture the thing for good, because of the limits of language and because every experience has its own difference and particularity. Just as no two people are the same, no two separations are made in precisely the same way.

Parting from a loved one can be painful even when it is only for a time. In the winter of 1611, the poet John Donne left his wife Anne for several months to travel on the Continent with his newfound patron, Sir Robert Drury. Donne's connection to Drury was important to his future, as he had been dismissed from his position in public service for his secret marriage to Anne, the daughter of the Chancellor of the Garter. The couple had been living in poverty for several years, and Anne was pregnant. "A Valediction: Forbidding Mourning" opens with a comparison between death and the parting of husband and wife:

> As virtuous men pass mildly away,
>   And whisper to their souls to go,
> Whilst some of their sad friends do say
>   The breath goes now, and some say, No:
>
> So let us melt, and make no noise,
>   No tear-floods, nor sigh-tempests move;
> 'Twere profanation of our joys
>   To tell the laity our love.

The first stanza describes the death of a virtuous man, who merely "whispers" to his soul to go as his breath grows faint. His dying is so mild that his friends cannot say for certain whether the breath is still there or not. The second stanza draws from this example the poet's injunction to his wife to hold back her tears: this is not an occasion for mourning, even if she might be as sad as the friends of the dying man. The remaining seven verses of the poem justify this proscription by means of the kind of elaborate metaphors that earned for authors like Donne the ironic name of "metaphysical poets." In the first, the poet claims that the love between him and his wife is not to be compared to that of "dull sublunary lovers": such lovers cannot bear to be separated because their love is based on the mere sensory experience of eyes, lips, and hands. The love of the poet and wife is made of a purer essence, so refined that they hardly know what it is, like the heavenly spheres surrounding the earth. Therefore, when they part, their love does not suffer a breach; rather it expands, "like gold to airy thinness beat." Though rarefied, the image evokes the wedding bands which unite husband and wife.

The second metaphor is drawn from the art of the draftsman. Donne argues that if his and his wife's souls are two, they are like the two legs of a compass. Her soul is the fixed foot, which stands in the center and turns in accordance with the movements of the other foot:

> And though it in the centre sit,
>   Yet when the other far doth roam,
> It leans and hearkens after it,
>   And grows erect, as that comes home.
>
> Such wilt thou be to me, who must,
>   Like th'other foot, obliquely run;
> Thy firmness makes my circle just,
>   And makes me end where I begun.

The center leg, fixed at the foot, leans out and attends to the wandering foot, but straightens as that foot returns. Anne's soul, the poet hopes, shall be like that fixed leg, parted from her husband on the surface, but remaining joined to him at a higher point, the apex of the compass. Her "firmness" will ensure the trueness of his trajectory, bringing him back when the circle is complete.

A valediction is a speech of leave-taking, here accompanied by an interdiction. But Donne attempts to soften the act of "forbidding" mourning with a series of arguments: he and his wife should emulate the virtue of the dying man who passes away peacefully; their love is so refined that it merely expands rather than breaking with their separation; they remain connected to each other like the two legs of a compass. These arguments are not consistent with one another: the dying man, however virtuous, cannot return to his friends; the gold, once expanded, can hardly resume its original density. There is an underlying desperation in Donne's array of images, as if he were grasping at different weapons in his poetic arsenal in the hope that one would create the desired effect. This impression carries the additional suggestion that the mourning Donne seeks to repress is as much his own as his wife's. Considered in this light, the intellectual abstractions of the poem become something more than cleverness; they acquire a certain pathos. We can understand them as symptoms of the poet's own suffering, and as gallant attempts to relieve that of his wife. In the end, it is impossible to forbid mourning. But Donne's poem is a brave attempt at it.

Donne's attempt to console his wife stands in sharp contrast to a poem of Lord Byron's that addresses a former lover in a tone of reproach. "When We Two Parted" was written in 1815 to Lady Frances Webster, with whom Byron had been in love in 1813 during his visits to Aston Hall in Yorkshire, where she lived with her husband. Byron's displeasure stems from the fact that since he parted ways with Lady Frances, she has bestowed her favors on members of the opposite sex almost as freely as Byron himself has done. In 1815, a rumor attached her to the Duke of Wellington, even as the general was marshalling his forces for the Battle of Waterloo. However hard this was for Byron to take, he remained a gentleman. The published version of the poem in 1816 is backdated to 1808 in order to protect Lady Frances's identity, and the poem itself reveals nothing of the actual circumstances in which the affair took place. The poem begins by remembering the scene of their parting two years earlier:

> When we two parted
> In silence and tears,
> Half broken-hearted
> To sever for years,
> Pale grew thy cheek and cold,
> Colder thy kiss;
> Truly that hour foretold
> Sorrow to this.

In Byron's memory, the sudden coldness of Lady Frances cast a chill on the moment in which the lovers were "half broken-hearted." The sorrow of that moment for him foretold the sorrow he feels at present. In addition, what he feels now is betrayal:

> Thy vows are all broken,
> And light is thy fame;
> I hear thy name spoken,
> And share in its shame.

That the poet claims to share in the "shame" of his lover's tarnished reputation is a sign of his humiliation as well as his jealousy and sorrow. He takes on a tone of resentment, regretting that he should ever have known his lover "too well," and grieving that she could have so deceived him. He closes with the question of what to do should they meet again after long years, and gives an answer which returns us to the sorrowful language of the poem's opening: "How should I greet thee? With silence and tears." Byron's wounded pride, as well as his judgment of Lady Frances, might have been softened by the fact that after their affair she named two of her children after him. The son she bore in 1815 was called Charles Byron, and a later son was christened George Gordon, Byron's given name.

Byron's poem to Lady Frances was published in the same year as a poem bidding farewell to his wife, in what became one of the most notorious separations recorded in modern literature. Byron had married the wealthy and virtuous Anne Isabella Milbanke in January 1815, largely to pay off his debts. The marriage was a disaster, marked by Byron's erratic behavior, combined with rumors of his bisexuality and of incestuous relations with his half-sister, Augusta. Lady Byron was driven from their home a year later, taking with her their infant daughter, Ada. Surrounded by scandal, Byron left for the continent in April 1816, after circulating among friends a poem of farewell to his wife. It is a deeply personal and moving work, though it oscillates between sincere affection and painful reproach. The ambivalence is manifest from the very first lines:

> Fare thee well! And if for ever,
> Still for ever, fare *thee well*!
> Even though unforgiving, never
> Gainst thee shall my heart rebel.

Byron plays on the double meaning of farewell: a final goodbye, and a wish for the other's welfare. In the next two lines, however, he diminishes the gesture of goodwill by describing his heart as "unforgiving" even if resigned to their separation. In succeeding lines, he reproaches his wife for "spurning" the breast on which her head had lain so often, and accuses her of having inflicted a "cureless wound." The poet finally turns to the figure of their child, wondering whether the little girl will ever be taught to say "Father." The truth is that he and Lady Byron were never to meet again, fulfilling the poem's prophecy that "both shall live," but that each will wake every morning to "a widow'd bed." The concluding lines strike a note of profound sadness in its evocation of their daughter:

> When her little hands shall press thee,
> When her lip to thine is press'ed,
> Think of him whose prayer shall bless thee,
> Think of him thy love had bless'd!

The poem as a whole testifies to the void left in the poet's life by the loss of his wife and child, and to his difficulty in accepting that loss, however responsible he may be for it.

"Fare Thee Well" was received sympathetically by the poet's friends, but his separation took on an entirely new dimension when the poem was pirated and published, both in newspaper and pamphlet form. Thus made public, "Fare Thee Well" was accompanied by another poem of Byron's on the dissolution of his marriage, entitled "A Sketch from Private Life." This latter work was a vitriolic attack on Lady Byron's confidante, Mrs. Clermont, whom he saw as instrumental in engineering the breakup. Mrs. Clermont is variously compared to Shakespeare's Iago, to a snake, a Gorgon, a "hag of hatred," a monster, and so on. Byron's barely contained resentment against his wife is given full force as it is unleashed on Lady Byron's friend.

The matter did not stop there. Beginning in the spring of 1816 and continuing for years, various pamphleteers took up Lady Byron's cause against her husband, publishing responses to "Fare Thee Well" either in their own names or in poems they falsely attributed to the Lady herself, such as "A Reply to Fare Thee Well!!! Lines Addressed to Lord Byron" (1816). The satirical cartoonist Isaac Cruickshank published an engraving entitled, "The separation, a sketch from the private life of Lord Iron [sic], who panegyrized his wife but satirized her confidante!!" The drawing shows Byron uttering the opening lines to "Fare Thee Well" with a dismissive gesture toward his wife and child at their house in Piccadilly Terrace. Byron has his arm around waist of Mrs. Mardyn, an actress and one of his mistresses, here dressed in extreme décolleté while gazing triumphantly at the scene. Mrs. Clermont is pictured as a misshapen old woman, looking daggers at the poet while taking her place alongside Lady Byron.

Byron was the first celebrity in the modern sense, and his private life was always public. He admits as much in "Fare Thee Well," where he acknowledges that "the world" will commend his wife for having spurned him, but that its favor should offend her, being "founded on another's woe." Byron could have foreseen that even as deeply personal a poem as "Fare Thee Well" would immediately find its way into the public sphere. Byron himself included it in his *Poems* of 1816. What it says about parting is that the pain can manifest itself in various ways, as sorrow, regret, and accusation. It attests to Byron's essential loneliness, a loneliness he sought, whether consciously or not, to alleviate by playing out his private drama on the public stage as it existed in the form of gossip, newspapers, pamphlets, and his own poems. But whatever the ruins of Byron's personal life, the poems are salvaged from them. He has made a lasting work out of his own ruin.

To turn from Byron to Emily Dickinson is to experience the literary equivalent of culture shock. It is go from a public to a private life, from the clamorous world of fame to one of quiet solitude, from relatively conventional poetic diction to one of often obscure intensity. She has written several poems about the pain of being apart from the one she loves, including some which are directly addressed to this person. No one knows for certain that person's identity, and theories abound. Dickinson lived in her father's house all her life; she never married, but late in life she gently rebuffed a proposal of marriage from Judge Otis Lord, a widower of her father's generation.

Her poems, however, testify to a passionate attachment, notably to the person she addressed as "Master," for whom several candidates have been proposed, including, as mentioned in an earlier chapter, the editor Samuel Bowles. However, in one of her poems the person addressed is described as having "served Heaven," suggesting a member of the clergy. One possibility is the Rev. Charles Wadsworth, a married Presbyterian minister from Philadelphia with whom Dickinson corresponded, and who visited her in Amherst in about 1860 before accepting a call to San Francisco the following year. By all available evidence, their relationship was never other than Platonic, even if marked by passionate feeling, at least on Dickinson's part. In the end it does not matter to whom Dickinson's love poems are addressed; what matters is their expression of how it feels to be separated from the object of one's love.

Dickinson did not date her poems, and so their chronological order has been based on material evidence such as changes in her handwriting and in the paper she used. According to this order, a poem written in about 1862, the year after Wadsworth's departure, is spoken in the voice of a woman who does not know when or even if she will see her lover again:

> If you were coming in the Fall,
> I'd brush the Summer by
> With half a smile, and half a spurn,
> As Housewives do, a Fly.
>
> If I could see you in a year,
> I'd wind the months in balls—
> And put them each in separate Drawers,
> For fear the numbers fuse—
>
> If only Centuries, delayed,
> I'd count them on my Hand,
> Subtracting, till my fingers dropped
> Into Van Dieman's Land.
>
> If certain, when this life was out—
> That yours and mine, should be
> I'd toss it yonder, like a Rind,
> And take Eternity—
>
> But, now, uncertain of the length
> Of this, that is between,
> It goads me, like the Goblin Bee—
> That will not state—its sting.

The first four stanzas entertain the possibility of a finite period of waiting for the lover's return, be it a season, a year, centuries from now, or in eternity, when their two lives will have ended. The poet could withstand any period of separation if she were sure that it would end in reunion with her lover. But she does not know if she will see him even after death, in Eternity. It is not the years but the uncertainty that she cannot endure. Even the absence of hope would be preferable to this condition. The brilliance of the poem lies in the way it presents this anguish in a framework that is both domestic and metaphysical, thus lending a tragic element to the simple life of "a woman of no importance," to borrow Oscar Wilde's phrase.

The images of the first two stanzas are drawn from the daily life of a woman occupied, as Dickinson was, with the upkeep of her father's house. The poem is set in summer, but with the promise of her lover's return she would brush the summer off like a fly. If it were a matter of months, those months could be wound up like balls of yarn and put in separate drawers to keep them from getting tangled, that is, to keep from losing count of the months. At this point the amplification of time is accompanied by that of space, so that the poet imagines herself able to reach across the globe to the antipodes (Van Dieman's Land, today Tasmania). Any given number of epochs would be "only Centuries" which she could count off on her fingers. And if certain that she would re-join her lover in eternity, she would cast off this life like the rind of a fruit. But the conclusion returns to present reality. Her uncertainty is likened to a "Goblin Bee" buzzing about her without deciding to sting. The assonant "o's" of "goads" and "Goblin" imitate the drone of the bee, while the opening consonants of "state" prepare for the final "sting" that menaces but does not come. It is a simple and natural image that nonetheless comes close to madness. The paradox of this metaphor is that the poet would welcome the sting, which, rather than give her pain, would restore her love. What the poem does not openly admit is the possibility that she will never see her lover again, in this life or the next.

Such is the unhappy conclusion to another poem written at about the same time, which is similarly organized: where "If you were coming in the Fall" entertains the thought of the lover's return at increasingly distant moments in the future, "I cannot live with you" considers, one by one, the reasons why she can never be united with her lover. This time, the question is posed in terms not of the duration of their separation, but rather in terms of life and death. It begins,

> I cannot live with You—
> It would be Life—
> And Life is over there—
> Behind the Shelf

In other words, the possibility of the two lovers living together has been permanently shelved, presumably by circumstances beyond their control. The shelf is the one "the Sexton keeps the key to." A sexton is the caretaker of a church's property, and the implication is that the life the poet cannot live with her lover, though sacred, has been put out of reach, like a cracked piece of porcelain discarded by a housewife. In a reference to a famous French dinnerware, the poet remarks, "A newer Sevres pleases—Old ones crack—." Her own love is too "Quaint—or Broke" to serve. In terms of the common objects of domestic life, she conveys the image of an ideal love unsuited to this world.

If the poet cannot live with her lover, then might she die with him? Here again the answer is no:

> I could not die—with You—
> For One must wait
> To shut the Other's Gaze down—
> You—could not—

He could not see her die, nor could she stand by and see him go without claiming her own right to die, her "Right of Frost." The idea is somewhat paradoxical: on one hand, the lovers cannot die together because one must wait to shut the other's eyes. On the other hand, she would not stand by to see her lover "freeze" without claiming the same fate, even if she were bound to wait to shut his eyes. Taken together, however, the lines convey the impossibility of a shared death, however that may be wished.

The second half of the poem takes us beyond life and death to an imagined ascent to heaven:

> Nor could I rise—with You—
> Because Your Face
> Would put out Jesus'—
> That New Grace
>
> Grow plain—and foreign
> On my homesick Eye—
> Except that You than He
> Shone closer by—

These lines, which verge on sacrilege, would be scandalous to Dickinson's church-going neighbors, as well as to the Rev. Charles Wadsworth were he ever to read them. The poet could not ascend to heaven with her lover because in her eyes he would outshine Jesus; the face of the savior would be plain and foreign to her unless illuminated by that of her lover. How would they be judged at heaven's gate? Her lover "served Heaven" or sought to, whereas she could not: her sight was so "saturated" by the aspect of him that she had no more eyes for the comparatively "sordid excellence" of mere heavenly paradise. But as to the final judgment, the poet fears their eternal separation. Were her lover to be "lost" to eternal perdition, she would be lost in a profounder sense, even if her name were loudly acclaimed in heaven. Were he saved and she condemned to be "where you were not," then "That Self—were Hell to me—."

Having exhausted the possibilities in life and death for the lovers' union, the poem reaches the inevitable conclusion:

> So We must meet apart—
> You there—I—here—
> With just the door ajar
> That oceans are—and Prayer—
> And that White Sustenance—
> Despair—

In what sense is despair a "white sustenance"? It is one of those formulations in Dickinson that seems stunningly apt for reasons that are difficult to say. We know that white was Dickinson's color. In Amherst, a newly arrived neighbor wrote to her family of Dickinson as the town's "myth": "She dresses wholly in white, and her mind is said to be perfectly wonderful." The Dickinson Homestead in Amherst displays her white dress; at her death the poet was buried in white and enclosed in a white casket. In various poems, the color white has the value of the absolute, as in the one that begins, "Dare you see a soul at the white heat?" Her favorite Bible verse was said to be Revelation 3:5, where God says to John, "He that overcometh, the same shall be clothed in white raiment." Here white is the color of divine election, as in several of Dickinson's poems, but also of suffering: "Of Tribulation, these are They, Denoted by the White." But Dickinson's "white sustenance" cannot be entirely explained by references to the Bible, since it is equated with despair, contrary to the Christian virtue of hope. It therefore seems possible that, denied the "salvation" of reunion with her lover on earth and in heaven, the poet devotes herself to the anti-faith of despair, in keeping with the heretical image of her lover's countenance outshining that of Jesus. More pious souls than she have been driven by despair to spiritual rebellion, there to find a measure of sustenance.

If we compare the earlier "If You were coming in the Fall" to "I cannot live with You," the latter poem has at least come to a definite conclusion after a systematic process of elimination: she can neither live, nor die, nor spend eternity with her lover. There is purity in absolute impossibility, a cold satisfaction in having arrived at the inevitability of absence—in abandoning all hope, like the damned souls in Dante. In *Either / Or*, Kierkegaard's monumental work on living an ethical life, despair is opposed to doubt. The difference is that one chooses despair, and that to do so is to affirm, however paradoxically, one's own validity: "You there—I—here," the "I" standing alone in the face of its own destiny. As sustenance, this is not enough to live on, but it may be enough for existence.

A little after these poems were written, Dickinson writes another in a tone of resignation. This poem claims a measure of reassurance in the mere fact that she and her lover are both alive on the same earth, even if they are never to meet again:

> So set its Sun in Thee
> What Day be dark to me—
> What distance—far—
>
> So I the Ships may see
> That touch—how seldomly—
> Thy Shore?

The emotion of the poem is made all the more powerful by the restraint of its monosyllables, the simplicity of its imagery and rhyme, and its extreme condensation—a pure distillation of feeling. The lovers' separation is evoked in time and space, respectively. The day, a measure of time, cannot be dark as long as its sun sets in the west, allowing her to travel, at least in imagination, to where her lover lives. Nor can the distance in space be far as long as she can see the ships that put in, however seldom, at the shore of her lover's country. The sun and the ships are figures for her thoughts, which voyage through time and space to dwell on her lover; he is present in them. This is not, however, a poem of satisfaction. The rhetorical question posed in the poem would seem to require the answer that no day is dark, no distance far given the voyages of the sun and the ships. Yet the tone is one of intense longing, for which the reach of the poet's thoughts are small consolation in the face of her loss. The dashes that separate "—far—" and "—how seldomly—" from what precedes and follows these words are graphic signs of a failure to overcome the limits imposed by time and space. The lover remains far off in space, and only "seldomly" is touched by the poet's thoughts.

Toward the end of her life Dickinson wrote a final poem on the subject of parting. This one looks back on two fatal events in her life, while contemplating the nature of death as a third:

> My life closed twice before its close—
> It yet remains to see
> If Immortality unveil
> A third event to me
>
> So huge, so hopeless to conceive
> As these that twice befell.
> Parting is all we know of heaven,
> And all we need of hell.

It is plausible to assume that the former "closings" in Dickinson's life were made by the departures of two persons to whom she was deeply attached, such as Charles Wentworth and Samuel Bowles. It hardly matters who; what matters is that for the poet these were moments when her life "closed." She wonders if death and "Immortality" will unveil a third event of the same magnitude. The second stanza casts doubt on this possibility: she cannot conceive that leaving life behind, even for immortality, could be as momentous as the two endings she has already put to her life. It is as if death could hardly put an end to her life, that life having ended already twice over. The poem concludes with an aphorism, where heaven is not paradise but rather that realm we enter after death; as for hell, it is the state of suffering. All we know of heaven is what we feel the loss of in being parted from the one we love. If heaven be more than this, it remains to be known. As for hell, we need no more of it—we can endure no more—than that which we suffer in parting. The poem's closing moves from the first person singular to the plural "we," making a general observation on parting as part of the human condition. Dickinson here stands back from purely personal testimony, in almost philosophical detachment at a moment when death is no longer to fear. The "we" of these lines is meant to include the reader, and to impart to us whatever truth she has gained from her loss.

Dickinson's sense of bewilderment at parting is shared by a more recent American poet, Louise Bogan. Bogan was briefly married to a soldier named Curt Alexander during the First World War. Although she bore a child, the marriage went badly, and was effectively over by 1918. His death in 1920 caused her to write a poem entitled "To a Dead Lover," published in the August 1922 issue of *Poetry* magazine with three other poems by Bogan under the title *Beginning and End*. Among them was the poem "Leave-Taking," apparently written when Alexander was still alive, on the subject of their separation. The poem conveys not just the poet's own sorrow, but also that of her departed lover:

> I do not know where either of us can turn
> Just at first, waking from the sleep of each other.
> I do not know how we can bear
> The river struck by the gold plummet of the moon,
> Or many trees shaken together in the darkness.
> We shall wish not to be alone
> And that love were not dispersed and set free—
> Though you defeat me,
> And I be heavy upon you.

At the moment of parting, or shortly thereafter, the poet predicts what life will be like for each of them, as Byron has done in addressing his estranged wife. "In the sleep of each other," Bogan and her husband have lived as in a dream, each unused to seeing the world alone. And so she wonders how each can bear the beauty of the earth without being able to share it with the other: the river in the gold light of moon, the trees shaking in darkness. In such moments they will wish, not exactly to be together again, but not to be alone. The lovers will be uneasy in the newfound freedom of their parting, despite their mutual strife, in which he "defeats" her, and her presence weighs on him.

The second part of the poem, symmetrical to the first in its nine lines, does not appeal for the lovers to be reunited. Rather, the poet remains committed to a love "perfect to the last," even if it takes the form of leave-taking:

> But like earth heaped over the heart
> Is love grown perfect.
> Like a shell over the beat of life
> Is love perfect to the last.
> So let it be the same
> Whether we turn to the dark or to the kiss of another;
> Let us know this for leavetaking,
> That I may not be heavy upon you,
> That you may blind me no more.

The first two similes convey the idea of "love grown perfect" in death and in life: in death, when earth is heaped over the heart in the grave, and in life, when a protective shell covers the beating heart. The images of death and life as alike preservers of love are then extended to the images of turning to "the dark" or to "the kiss of another." In either case, the love made perfect remains so to the last. In a final gesture, the poet appeals to her lover to understand their parting as one more act of love, so that she may no longer weigh heavily on him, perhaps as a source of guilt, and he will no longer blind her, thus allowing her to see beyond him. The wisdom of this gesture tells us that she is in fact no longer blind; as for her "defeat," the poem itself succeeds in saving love from that, even if it fails to bring the lovers back together. A poem which begins in the confusion of not knowing has made its way toward a new kind of knowledge, gained at the cost of parting.

What all these poems have to show us is that parting is not one thing. What we call parting has been defined in many ways, and poets find creative ways of confronting, suffering, and transforming the experience. Donne resorts to a series of inventive metaphors to "forbid" his wife from mourning his departure, while the impression he gives of straining for effect does little to provide reassurance. Byron's bitterness at parting is an unsuccessful attempt to transfer blame from himself to his wife, while his poem serves as eloquent testimony to his own loneliness. Dickinson engages in a desperate search for relief from the pain of parting, followed by progressive attempts to live within the constraints of diminished possibilities. Bogan attempts to transform the pain of parting into a liberating act of love. Parting may be all we need of hell, but among these poems there may be help in surviving it.

Dejection

In "Mourning and Melancholia," Freud is at pains to distinguish between these two unhappy states. Whereas mourning is a natural response to the loss of a loved one, the cause of melancholy is not so clear: one cannot see precisely what it is that has been lost, and yet the melancholy person suffers from many of the same symptoms as the mourner: lack of interest in the outside world, loss of the ability to love, the absence of desire for any activity whatsoever. In addition to these misfortunes, the melancholic suffers from a lowering of self-regard that manifests itself in self-reproach and an impoverishment of the sense of the value of the self. The melancholic is finally puzzling to Freud because "we cannot see what it is that is absorbing him so entirely."

The most basic distinguishing feature of melancholy, says Freud, is "profoundly painful dejection." Freud's translator Lytton Strachey has chosen this latter word as an approximate equivalent to the German *Verstimmung*, which one could also translate as "ill humor," or "ill feeling." Strachey is no doubt sensitive to the resonance of "dejection" in English poetry. The concepts of melancholy, dejection, and depression in fact follow a roughly historical order in their relative degrees of currency. In Shakespeare's day melancholy had a physiological origin. It was thought to be caused by an excess of "black bile," one of the four principal fluids that constitute one's "humor," or temperament. Dejection, literally the fact of being cast down, gained currency as a word during the Romantic era of the late eighteenth and early nineteenth centuries. With the rise of psychology in the twentieth century, "dejection" gave way in turn to "depression" as an object of medical treatment. I shall use the more literary "dejection," but whatever it is called, the symptoms and the obscure nature of its cause remain the same. What I wish to show is that poets offer some relief from this kind of suffering.

The most famous English poem on dejection was written by Coleridge in 1802, when he was 30. He had married reluctantly in 1794 as part of a scheme to create a utopian community in America, but the plan had fallen through, leaving Coleridge living unhappily with his wife and children. To make matters worse, he had fallen in love with the sister of Wordsworth's future wife, Sara Hutchinson, whom he met occasionally near his home in the Lake District of England. This doomed attachment was accompanied by an illness doubtless aggravated by Coleridge's addiction to opium. In addition to these misfortunes, he felt that he had lost his imaginative power as a poet. It was in this state of mind that he wrote a verse letter to Sara, which he later reworked into "Dejection: An Ode." The poem is written in eight sections, but can be read as three main movements, respectively, of outward observation, inward contemplation, and a sense of recovery.

In the first of these movements the poet gazes out on a tranquil night, but senses an approaching storm. He longs for the "coming on of rain and squally blast" to arouse him from his feelings of torpor:

> A grief without a pang, void, dark, and drear,
> A stifling, drowsy, unimpassioned grief,
> That finds no natural outlet, no relief
> In word or sigh, or tear—

It is a "heartless mood" whose obscure origin and uncertain object prevent the poet from putting it into words and even from weeping. Looking out on the western sky, the stars, the crescent moon and the blue lake, he sees how "excellently fair" are these natural forms, but to his dismay their beauty leaves him unmoved: "I *see*, not *feel*, how beautiful they are!"

The second movement of the poem turns to an inward reflection on the reasons for this absence of feeling in the presence of natural beauty, uncharacteristic of a poet who, in poems like "Frost at Midnight," has written so memorably of the inspiration to be derived from nature. Here he despairs of finding consolation in outward forms:

> Though I should gaze forever
> On that green light that lingers in the west—
> I may not hope from outward forms to win
> The passion and the life, whose fountains are within!

The spirits of the poet cannot be raised by outward influence. He has come to believe that "we receive but what we give," and that whatever we experience of beauty or of joy in nature, in things such as the light and the luminous cloud which now envelop the earth—that beauty must issue from the soul itself, "of its own birth." Nature is nothing without this power of the soul to create beauty, which Coleridge calls joy. That joy is something he can remember from earlier life, but now "afflictions bow me down to earth"; they suspend "my shaping spirit of imagination"—another way of defining the soul's power to make beauty.

In a final movement, the poet consciously banishes these thoughts as he turns again to the window, beyond which the storm now rages. There follow violent images of raving wind and blasted trees, as if the storm were staging a scene of war, complete with an army fleeing in retreat, "with groans, of trampled men, with smarting wounds." And then, in a sudden lull, the storm abates, with "sounds less deep and loud." There are groans and shudderings which announce its end, while they also seem to tell another tale—of a lonely child who has lost her way in the wild, and who calls out for her mother in grief and fear. In both of these examples, Coleridge attributes an imaginative faculty to the storm—"Thou Actor [...] Thou mighty Poet," whereas it is his own imagination that is at work. The source of the terrible beauty in nature is within him, such that, for at least as long as the storm lasts, his imaginative power is restored.

But this momentary inspiration is not enough for lasting relief from dejection. That can be reached only by way of love for another. Already during the storm he has pictured the suffering of others: the wounded soldiers in retreat, the lost little girl. In other words, although his imagination has its source within his own soul, its creative power can be restored only through a movement outward to the souls of others. The conclusion of the poem thus leaves the poet's afflictions behind in order to bestow a blessing on the woman he loves. It is midnight, the storm is passed. The final lines take the form of a prayer to "gentle Sleep" to visit his love with "wings of healing":

> May all the stars hang bright above her dwelling,
> Silent as though they watched the sleeping Earth!
> With light heart may she rise,
> Gay fancy, cheerful eyes,
> Joy lift her spirit, joy attune her voice;
> To her may all things live, from pole to pole,
> Their life the eddying of her living soul!
> O simple spirit, guided from above,
> Dear Lady! friend devoutest of my choice,
> Thus may thou ever, evermore rejoice.

The prayer is addressed to the spirit of Sleep rather than to God, but it is still a prayer, an appeal beyond the self that turns to a greater power. The beauty of the night, which before the poet could see but not feel, now stirs his feelings of benevolence and love. The joy he claimed to have lost he now wishes for his lover, a joy here defined as the eddying, or circular current, of her soul. The image is of a soul from which life issues forth to all things, which itself finds joy in living things. When the poet wishes that his lover might "evermore rejoice," the feeling itself is at least a potential source of joy to the poet in that he can now imagine the lasting joy of his love. That thought is one in which the poet himself can rejoice. Coleridge's poem as a whole enacts a great eddying movement, joining the poet's soul to the natural world and to the soul of other human beings. It points the way toward relief from dejection in the soul's power to both generate and give way to that current: "we receive but what we give."

In Coleridge the inability to feel is one of the symptoms of dejection, which in turn entails the loss of imaginative power. The paradox is that dejection itself is a kind of feeling, even as "passionless grief," and that dejection can be the subject of a work of imagination such as an ode. The very feeling that subdues imagination thus becomes the source of inspiration, as if the poet's innate powers sought to revolt against their own oppression. For poets of the Romantic period, the absence of traditional religious faith made them seek consolation from misfortune in their own creative powers, even if those powers enabled no more than the poetic expression of dejection. Suffering must find expression. The poet's suffering is alleviated by being named and objectified, and above all by making it something that others can understand. Something like this is taking place in Percy Shelley's "Stanzas Written in Dejection, near Naples."

Shelley has consciously chosen Coleridge's word for his title, and as in the older poet's case, a host of reasons contributed to Shelley's feeling of dejection. His poem was written in December 1818, when he and his wife Mary were spending the winter in Naples. Shelley was in ill health, but had other cause for unhappiness. In September, his infant daughter Clara had died in Venice; she had been ill with dysentery and the journey there may have hastened her death. Two years earlier Shelley's first wife, Harriet, had committed suicide, and he had lost custody of their children. Another girl had just been born in Naples and registered as Shelley's daughter, but not by Mary. It is not known whether this was an adopted child or Shelley's illegitimate daughter; in the latter case, it would have been an additional source of anxiety. Finally, Shelley felt that his literary career was a failure. In Mary's notes later published with his poems, she writes of this period, "His thoughts, shadowed by illness, became gloomy,—and then he escaped to solitude, and in verses, which he hid from fear of wounding me, poured forth morbid but too natural bursts of discontent and sadness."

Shelley's stanzas begin, like Coleridge's ode, by looking out on the landscape, but at noon rather than at night, and on the dazzling bay of Naples: the unusually warm December sun, a clear sky, the bright, dancing waves of the sea. He sits alone on the sand, where the waves on the shore make their sound of "measured motion," and like Coleridge, he witnesses the beauty of the scene without feeling it: "How sweet! did any heart now share in my emotion." This reflection signals the poem's inward turn, where the poet discloses the nature of his dejection:

> Alas! I have nor hope nor health,
> Nor peace within nor calm around,
> Nor that content surpassing wealth
> The sage in meditation found,
> And walked with inward glory crowned—
> Nor fame, nor power, nor love, nor leisure.

As he expresses it, many things are lacking in the poet's life: hope, health, peace, calm, fame, power, love, and leisure. We know this not to be entirely true, for we have evidence of Shelley's growing reputation as a poet, and the unequivocal testimony of Mary's love. But in his dejection Shelley feels none of this. He seems particularly to regret the absence of contentment which the wise find in meditation, a serenity surpassing material wealth.

All these things are to be desired, but in despair of ever having them the poet finds another object of desire, and that is death. The mildness of the wind and waters before him lead him to feel that he could welcome death as benign, like a child crying itself to sleep:

> I could lie down like a tired child,
> And weep away the life of care
> Which I have borne and yet must bear,
> Till death like sleep might steal on me,
> And I might feel in the warm air
> My cheek grow cold, and hear the sea
> Breathe o'er my dying brain its last monotony.

Like Keats listening to the nightingale's song, Shelley is "half in love with easeful death," a gentle dying in which he would still feel the warm air and hear the sea. Having thus imagined his death, Shelley now speculates on how it would make others feel. The final stanza begins with the thought that "Some might lament that I were cold," and ends with these lines:

> They might lament—for I am one
> Whom men love not,—and yet regret,
> Unlike this day, which, when the sun
> Shall on its stainless glory set,
> Will linger, though enjoyed, like joy in memory yet.

Only some "might" lament the poet's death, for many disapproved of his life. Shelley was much blamed for his atheism, his radical views, his doctrine of free love, and so on. This ambivalent "regret" at the poet's end stands in stark contrast to the feeling engendered by the end of this mild and sunny day. Unlike the poet's scandal-ridden life, the sun will set in "stainless glory" over the sea. And unlike the unloved poet, the day, once passed, will linger on in memory as a source of joy. If Shelley has reasons for feeling dejected by the circumstances of his life, the prospects for his afterlife only add to those reasons. And yet the poem ends on a note, however tentative, of joy. The sweetness of the day, which at first failed to move his heart, has made despair itself mild; in the midst of despair, he has found joy in nature, and he knows that this joy will last beyond the day's end. It is not much in the way of relieving the poet's dejection, but it is nonetheless a recognition that his "lost heart" is lost amid a world of gentle beauty. The view over the sea is one of eternity, as is the image of the setting sun. In Shelley's thought, this realm is infinitely greater than that of the self in this sad world.

It is worth pointing out that when Shelley wrote his stanzas on dejection, he was in the midst of writing *Prometheus Unbound*, a much more ambitious work in which the apprehension of beauty is a necessary condition for a peaceful world on earth. It was in this context that Yeats read Shelley's more despairing work: "Shelley [...] found compensation for his 'loss,' for the taking away of his children, for his quarrel with his first wife, for later sexual disappointment, for his exile, for his obloquy—there were but three or four persons, he said, who did not consider him a monster of iniquity—in his hopes for the future of mankind." In other words, the ultimate consequence of Shelley's dejection was, somewhat paradoxically, an ethical impulse based on love for his fellow human beings. Shelley's stanzas on dejection are also about the perception of beauty, and in his system of thought that perception is a manifestation of love. The poet's soul, then, finds in all forms of beauty an ideal order which his spirit longs for in the order of human life. That order is the freedom of souls who love one another. In this way, Shelley writes in a prose fragment, we "seek to awaken in all things that are, a community with what we experience within ourselves." It is this philosophy that, according to Mary Shelley, made her husband hesitate as to whether he should be a metaphysician or a poet.

In the year 1916, Yeats was similarly torn between a metaphysical, even mystical system of thought and a desire to write as the poetic voice of Ireland, then emerging as a new nation. The Easter Rising in Dublin of April 1916, when Irish nationalists rebelled against British rule, forced a crisis in the way Yeats saw his vocation. He sought to respond to the events of April by writing his magisterial "Easter, 1916," which celebrates the memory of the 16 men executed for their part in their rebellion, a martyrdom out of which "a terrible beauty is born." The violence of these events called for the poet's attention to the changing world around him, away from his absorption in dreamlike images of the supernatural. In September 1916, just as Yeats was finishing "Easter, 1916," he wrote "Lines Written in Dejection," its title adapted from Shelley. It is a direct expression of the crisis in the meaning and purpose of his poetry:

> When have I last looked on
> The round green eyes and the long wavering bodies
> Of the dark leopards of the moon?
> All the wild witches, those most noble ladies,
> For all their broom-sticks and their tears,
> Their angry tears, are gone.
> The holy centaurs of the hills are vanished;
> I have nothing but the embittered sun;
> Banished heroic mother moon and vanished,
> And now that I have come to fifty years
> I must endure the timid sun.

The moon, the leopards, the witches and centaurs—all these are images of a fanciful world which Yeats half-believed existed in the form of "elemental powers" behind the world we know objectively. In any case, he had given them an important place in the universe of his poetic imagination. What the poem announces, with a certain regret, is the end of this mystical business: the holy centaurs are banished, as is the heroic mother moon. It has been some time since the poet has looked to them for inspiration. In their absence, what is left is the "embittered sun": the world of visible reality, a "timid sun" in its meagre power to stir the poet's imagination. The poem is not just one of dejection, but also of renunciation.

What then is the importance of the poet's age, "come to fifty years"? A possible answer is that he associates the aging of his body with a certain loss of imaginative power. This explanation hardly corresponds with reality, however, for in 1816 Yeats was at the height of his powers as a poet. A more likely reason is that maturity in years, combined with recent historical events, has led him to renounce the style of a youthful poetic imagination with all its mystical figures. This explanation is borne out by some of the other poems published with "Lines Written in Dejection" in the volume *The Wild Swans at Coole* (1919). In a poem called "The Fisherman," Yeats expresses his desire to write "for my own race and the reality," a poem "as cold And passionate as the dawn" in the image of the "wise and simple man" of the poem's title. Yeats, we remember, thought Shelley found compensation for his dejection in another kind of poetry dedicated to the ideal of universal love. Possibly, at a certain moment of his life, Shelley's poem of dejection was a necessary condition for the later poetry of idealism, as if his attraction to death made him realize the importance of life. In similar manner, Yeats's poem of dejection, in marking the dead end of his mysticism, prepares the way for a new kind of poetic vocation, the desire to write for the wise and simple man in his "grey Connemara clothes" fishing in the light of dawn. Yeats's way out of dejection is to realize that the calling of this world is a higher one than that of his mystical paradise.

A key to Freud's distinction between mourning and melancholia is that in the latter, the cause of dejection cannot be located in a particular loss. Mourning is a natural response to the pain of loss, but the symptoms of melancholia, or dejection, appear to be beyond pain: in Coleridge's words, "a grief without a pang." Pain hurts, but it is at least a form of suffering on which we can concentrate our efforts to resist it. It finds a natural outlet in tears and cries. Dejection, however, has no such natural outlet, and must be expressed in art. Shelley's response to it is a death-wish, while the speaker in Yeats's poem resigns himself to a diminished life of mere endurance. These two poets can at least attribute their dejection to what they lack: hope, health, and peace of mind in Shelley's case, imaginative power in Yeats's. Emily Dickinson has no use for such attributions, because she wants to convey, as closely as it is possible to do so in words, the state of mind itself:

> There is a Languor of the Life
> More imminent than Pain—
> 'Tis Pain's Successor—When the Soul
> Has suffered all it can—

> A Drowsiness—diffuses—
> A Dimness like a Fog
> Envelops Consciousness—
> As Mists—obliterate a Crag.
>
> The Surgeon—does not blanch—at pain
> His Habit—is severe—
> But tell him that it ceased to feel—
> The Creature lying there—
>
> And he will tell you—skill is late—
> A Mightier than He—
> Has ministered before Him—
> There's no Vitality.

Among the things that distinguish this poem is the absence of any explicit reference to the poet's life. There is no "I" in the poem, only the description of a state which others could feel as well. In the place of subjective confession, Dickinson puts herself in a relatively objective position regarding what one assumes to be her own experience. She conducts a kind of self-diagnosis, all the more powerful in its seemingly dispassionate analysis.

What Dickinson calls languor is similar to what Coleridge calls dejection: there is the same drowsiness and lack of feeling. But Dickinson probes more deeply, while also widening the perspective: the languor is "of the Life," and therefore not conditioned by particular circumstances in that life. It is neither pain nor suffering; it is "more imminent" than pain, meaning both more immediate and more intimate. Nor is it exactly suffering, but rather something like the exhaustion of suffering, and the void left in its place. The second stanza echoes the "drowsiness" of Coleridge's poem. Like Coleridge, she uses metaphors of weather, but the difference in Dickinson is that the atmospheric conditions of dejection are interior to the soul, if only metaphorically: a fog envelops consciousness the way mists obscure a mountain crag. The cragginess of consciousness, we might surmise, consists in its qualities of hardness, sharpness, and topographical relief—all obliterated by this languor.

In the second half of the poem the diagnosis is followed by a prognosis, this time by introducing a member of the medical profession. The surgeon is used to seeing pain, but if you tell him that the patient has ceased to feel, he will tell you that it is too late for him to intervene. As in many other Dickinson poems, there is a splitting of the poet's self: on one hand, she is the "Creature" lying there without feeling—even without humanity, as the designation "creature" implies; on the other hand, she is the poet herself, hearing the surgeon's hopeless prognosis. But the dialogue with the surgeon is not just her own; it could belong to any similar case, and this detachment enforces the objective, almost scientific tone of the poem. We are not told the name of the being mightier than the surgeon who has attended before him, but since it has taken away the creature's vitality, let us call it death.

We remember that in poems like "My life closed twice before its close," death for Dickinson can end the will to live before the end of life itself. What the poem offers by way of an antidote to the condition it describes is itself: the poem is not the mere expression of languor but rather an analysis which succeeds in gaining a critical distance on the absence of feeling that is its subject. The form of the poem, moreover, is anything but languorous: it is a disciplined alternation of four and three-stressed lines, with a consistent rhyme of the second and fourth line of each stanza. The rigor inherent in this form, combined with a striking use of metaphor, supplies the vitality of language necessary to define the destructive power of a languor more imminent than pain. This language finally lends to the poem an authenticity and an intimacy with the reader, who may have known this languor or witnessed it in others.

As we see in the poems discussed above, what is common to the various forms of dejection is a certain powerlessness—to feel, to hope, to create. These kinds of despair may be symptoms of something equally paralyzing and universal to the human condition, and that is the fear of death. With characteristic irony, Philip Larkin writes a poem on this fear in the form of an *aubade*—traditionally a song heralding the dawn. His poem begins before dawn, however, in a moment of awakened panic at four in the morning. In the first part of the poem, flawlessly arranged in ten lines of rhymed iambic meter, the poet awakens before dawn to stare into the darkness.

At this point one begins to realize the irony of the poem's title. The *aubade* has its origins in the middle ages. Traditionally, it is sung below the window of the poet's lover as a morning counterpart to the evening serenade. Or, if the poet has had the happiness of spending the night with his love, the *aubade* signals their urgent need to separate at the approaching dawn. The most famous *aubade* in English is the rhyming dialogue between Shakespeare's Romeo and Juliet, where she attempts to convince him that the birdsong heard outside is that of the nocturnal nightingale, not the morning lark. Romeo is not taken in by this pretty deceit: "If I want to live, I must go. If I stay, I'll die" (III.5). In Larkin's poem there is no lover, and the thought of death is quite other than Romeo's. Larkin was a solitary man, a librarian at a provincial English university. He wrote this poem at the age of 55 in 1977, a few years before his death from cancer. The first line of the poem, like the rest, is conversational in tone, but the powerful condensation of its language captures an existence lived out in quiet desperation. The sudden awakening at four o'clock is to darkness and silence, and as the sleepless poet waits for dawn to break, he sees in the soundless dark what is always there, the "unresting death" that awaits him always and everywhere, and to which the morning brings him one day nearer. He is himself unrestful at this moment, unable to think of anything except the when and where of his death. This "arid interrogation" does not dispel the dread, which "flashes afresh to hold and horrify." The one line that does not reach the full five stresses of iambic meter is the ninth, its three beats sounding out a pre-dawn knell: "Of dying, and being dead."

The flash of dread appears in the next stanza as a blinding glare at which the mind turns blank. This feeling is neither that of remorse for the wrongs the poet has committed, nor is it even wretchedness at the way his life has turned out. It is rather the frightening apprehension of the "total emptiness for ever" of what follows life:

> Not to be here,
> Not to be anywhere,
> And soon; nothing more terrible, nothing more true.

What comes after life, then, is precisely nothing, and the philosopher might say that therefore there is nothing to be afraid of. But that is not how this poem goes: the "sure extinction that we travel to" makes for "a special way of being afraid." In the last quarter of the twentieth century, the age-old means of dispelling this fear no longer work. Not religion, "that vast moth-eaten musical brocade" created precisely to pretend we never die. Not reason, which would claim that something we neither see nor hear cannot be the cause of fear. For the poet it is precisely this absence of sight, sound, sense, thought, and love that "we fear"—extending the dread beyond himself to ourselves as well. Here he joins Coleridge and Dickinson in defining a state bereft of feeling, with the difference that this time it is for ever: death is the "anaesthetic from which none come round."

Among the living, this anesthetic state is the consequence of an imperfect repression, in which the fear of death stays on the edge of consciousness as a paralyzing presence, a "standing chill That slows each impulse down to indecision." But the fear can blow both hot and cold. Like Dickinson, Larkin conveys in the most vivid terms the bodily effects of certain states of mind. When we are caught without the distractions of other people or of drink, the realization of death's certainty "rages out In furnace-fear"—a startling image of the hot flash one literally feels at such moments. Like religion and reason, even courage is powerless to avoid the approaching emptiness: "Death is no different whined at than withstood."

The poem's final lines return to the place the poem began, the poet's bedroom, where the light of dawn begins to break. The room, now visible, "stands plain as a wardrobe." The matter-of-factness of the wardrobe is an image of the plain truth, which "we can't escape Yet can't accept." One of these impossible alternatives—to escape or to accept the reality of death—will have to go, and there is little mystery as to which it will be. Meanwhile, the world around the poet is astir. But given his consciousness of doom, life goes on only under the bleakest of circumstances:

> The sky is white as clay, with no sun.
> Work has to be done.
> Postmen like doctors go from house to house.

This conclusion echoes a poem by Baudelaire called "Crépuscule du matin" or "Morning twilight," in which the Paris of the exhausted, cold and hungry, of the sick and dying, awakens under a heavy gray sky. In Larkin's scene the sky is similarly sunless over a "rented world," suggesting both the impermanence of life in rented lodgings and the fact that life itself is not "owned" by us in perpetuity: at some point the lease is up. Nonetheless, "Work has to be done": the single trimeter line among the longer pentameters falls like the certainty of death itself. If the postmen's rounds from house to house seem like those of doctors, it is because, given its fate, the life of every house is a sickness unto death.

Taken at face value, Larkin's poem could hardly be more depressing. But without denying its truth, there is reason to feel relieved, if not exactly cheered by it. Larkin penetrates the anesthetic that blunts the edges of life and traps us in willed forgetfulness. He rips away the veil of existence, faces directly our deepest fears, and finds words for them. This is already something, to have captured the great fear in this way, to have brought into focus a feeling both insidious and elusive. The other reason to celebrate this poem is for its mastery of the craft. The lines are rhymed, but the style is so natural that we hardly notice the rhyme. They are of equal, pentameter length, but again in a rhythm seemingly so effortless that it does not call attention to itself. The exception is the ninth line of each stanza, its truncated three-stress clang disrupting the natural flow of the poem, like a merciless reminder of death. What the poem does is to announce that death, and thus to make the life lived under its sentence more honest, more authentic, truer both to life and death.

What is worse: to be afraid of dying or to want to die? The former is a universal fear which we ignore by thinking of other things, even if it remains on the edge of our vision. The wish to die is something else. In contrast to Larkin, the poets of the Romantic period often wrote of death as a welcome release from sorrow. In the "Ode to a Nightingale," Keats muses on hearing the nightingale's song, "Now more than ever seems it rich to die, To cease upon the midnight with no pain." The feeling described is like Shelley's desire to "lie down like a tired child [...] Till death like sleep might steal on me." In both cases, the poet's spirits are cast down by circumstances in their lives. As we have seen, Shelley lacked hope, health, and contentment. As for Keats, he had just watched his brother die of tuberculosis, and was soon to die of the same disease. His is a world "Where youth grows pale, and spectre-thin, and dies; Where but to think is to be full of sorrow." But these death-wishes are different from one relatively independent of circumstance, and which belongs to the very nature of the person expressing it. Such is the desire given voice in Anne Sexton's "Wanting to Die."

Sexton suffered from a severe depressive illness never precisely diagnosed, much less resolved. Among its symptoms were psychological breakdowns, occasional trances, and suicidal tendencies. As a suburban housewife in the 1950s, she joined a poetry-writing class in Boston at the suggestion of her psychiatrist, who recognized her creative potential. He thought that it would help her, and others suffering from depression, to write about her experiences in treatment. In Diane Middlebrook's biography of Sexton, Dr. Martin Orne is quoted as saying to his patient, "You can't kill yourself, you have something to give. Why, if people read your poems, they would think 'There's somebody else like me.' They wouldn't feel alone." Sexton took his advice, and went on to become one of the finest poets of her generation. In 1967, she won the Pulitzer Prize for her collection *Live or Die*, which included the poem "Wanting to Die." It begins as if in the middle of a conversation with someone to whom the desire for death needs to be explained. The poet says that for her it becomes an "almost unnameable lust," even though she has nothing against life itself: the grass, the furniture placed under the sun. Suicides like her, however, have a special language:

> Like carpenters they want to know *which tools*.
> They never ask *why build*.

The poet speaks of two suicide attempts she has made, possessing and eating "the enemy," then resting, "heavy and thoughtful." The images recall the drug overdoses Sexton did indeed take. Again she speaks for suicidal persons as a class. Suicides, she says, are sometimes "still-born," meaning "they don't always die," but they still cannot forget "a drug so sweet that even children would look on and smile." The desire to swallow the deadly drug "becomes a passion": "To thrust all that life under your tongue!" The closing lines of the poem personify Death as one patiently waiting for the poet's release from life.

In Sexton's conceit, Death is a faithful lover, hurt by the poet's unsuccessful attempts to join her, yet still there for the moment when the poet will come. The ancient image of breath appears as the essence of life which death takes away. In Keats's "Ode to a Nightingale," Death is a figure whom the poet softly calls "To take into the air my quiet breath." In Sexton's poem Death waits "to empty my breath from its bad prison," the body. From this personal confession she returns to the subject of suicides in general, "balanced there" between life and death. The state of always being on the point of leaving is rendered in images of deception, frustration, and things left undone at the moment of self-inflicted death:

> leaving the page of the book carelessly open,
> something unsaid, the phone off the hook
> and the love, whatever it was, an infection.

Sexton's meaning here is unbearably sad, and it goes against the entire tradition of love in Western poetry. The love of others—her family, her friends—is not denied. But it was, if it was anything, an infection transmitted by life itself, like the old wound that death will undo when the poet is finally freed from her prison.

Despite Sexton's success as a poet, her story does not have a happy ending. In 1974, at the age of 45, she made her escape. She had dismissed her husband from her life, had alienated her friends and her therapist. To combat the loneliness, she drank heavily and took up brief affairs with strangers. At home one evening in suburban Boston, she went into the garage, closed the doors, and turned on the car engine until she went to sleep for good. As Martin Orne had assured her two decades earlier, Sexton had a great deal to give her readers, and she gave it. What distinguishes her poetry from mere self-expression, and what gives it its power, is its formal discipline. Her poems are as highly crafted as that of any poet. Evidence is to be found in her manuscripts, covered with meticulous notations of syllable counts and rhyme schemes. Middlebrook calls it "forcing discipline upon madness," and Sexton herself told an audience in 1968, "Poetry led me by the hand out of madness. I am hoping I can show others that route." Although she writes about suicide, Sexton believed that poetry was the opposite of suicide: a creative rather than a destructive act. She pointed out, for example, that if her poem called "Suicide Note" had been a real suicide note, she would not have put it through so many drafts. Among all the poets who have written of melancholy, dejection, and depression, Sexton speaks with particular authenticity as a witness to the most dire situation, the limit of existence at the knife edge between life and death. To justify her work, she liked to quote a line from a letter by Franz Kafka, which has meaning for all art, including poetry: "A book should serve as the axe for the frozen sea within us."

Self-Reliance

Ralph Waldo Emerson's essay on "Self-Reliance" enquires into the nature of the self as the foundation for judgment and the conduct of life. For Emerson, the essence of the self is in its spontaneity or instinct which, in its apprehension of the world, takes the form of a "primary wisdom" he calls intuition. This intuition is inherently superior to all other teachings. As the self possesses its own intuition, so the self is unique both in its constitution and its experience: no other is made the same way or has lived the same life. This is one more reason to trust yourself above others in their judgments and opinions, provided that you are truly attentive to your own instinct and intuition. Writing in 1841, Emerson extends the lessons of self-reliance beyond the individual to include the society and culture of his time; they seem especially relevant today. The pressure to conform in all things exposes the weakness of a society "afraid of truth, afraid of fortune, afraid of death," whose members are "afraid of each other." The virtue of self-reliance should likewise free the American artist from slavish imitation of European models. Instead, the artist should "study with hope and love the precise thing to be done by him" considering the climate, the landscape, the people, and the government of his own country. Only in this way will the artist create truly original work of taste and feeling. Emerson's model throughout his essay is that of nature, where "the bended tree recovering from the strong wind," like all other living creatures, is a demonstration of the self-relying soul. Finally, he finds in self-reliance a source of strength against misfortune and suffering: "Regret calamities, if it can help the sufferer; if not, attend to your own work, and already the evil begins to be repaired. [...] The secret of fortune is joy in our hands."

Emerson was a great reader of Wordsworth. The two poets met in 1833, when Emerson made the journey to Rydal Mount to see the older poet, then in his sixties. Among the poems by Wordsworth that could have inspired "Self-Reliance" is one written in 1802, when the poet was 32. It is called "Resolution and Independence." Like many poems of Wordsworth, this one tells a story that begins with a description of the landscape. In the aftermath of a storm at night the sun has risen, and the birds are singing in the woods:

> All things that love the sun are out of doors;
> The sky rejoices in the morning's birth;
> The grass is bright with raindrops; on the moors
> The Hare is running races in her mirth;
> And with her feet she from the plashy earth
> Raises a mist; which, glittering in the sun,
> Runs with her all the way, wherever she doth run.

The scene illustrates the spontaneity of self-reliance in nature, whose creatures obey their instincts and find joy in the present moment. The poet here appears as a "traveler upon the moor" who, at first delighted by the scene, soon sinks into dejection and despair. He cannot share the joy he sees in nature, so possessed is he by fears of future "solitude, pain of heart, distress, and poverty." Poetry is a risky career choice even in the best of circumstances, and Wordsworth was about to be married. He cites examples of other poets who have come to grief: Thomas Chatterton, the "marvellous boy" who, poor and lacking recognition, killed himself at the age of 17; Robert Burns, said to have hastened his death at 37 through drink, left his wife and children without support:

> We poets in our youth begin in gladness;
> And thereof come in the end despondency and madness.

This reflection leads back to the present scene, and to a turning point in the story, introduced in the manner of an epiphany: "by peculiar grace, A leading from above, a something given." Yet what is revealed is merely the figure of a very old man looking fixedly into a pond in the midst of the "naked wilderness." To the poet's rich imagination, the old man appears like a marvel of nature: a huge stone perched on a height, or a sea-beast having crawled forth to rest in the sun. The man stirs the surface of the pond with his staff, searching its depth "as if he had been reading in a book." The poet ventures to address him with what seems a casual remark: "This morning gives us promise of a glorious day." The remainder of the poem gives these words greater meaning than those of casual comment on the weather.

Encouraged by the old man's gentle reply, the poet asks, "What kind of work is that which you pursue?" The answer, though simple in the extreme, proves to be providential for the poet. What he first remarks is the old man's manner of expression, in which the poet finds a kind of natural poetry: words follow one another "in solemn order": "Choice word, and measured phrase; above the reach Of ordinary men; a stately speech!" The man has come to the pond to gather leeches, used in those days for medicinal purposes. He roams from pond to pond upon the moors, lodging by chance wherever he can. The poet finds this demonstration of plain and humble courage deeply moving: "Employment hazardous and wearisome!" The man has endured much hardship, yet "in this way he gained an honest maintenance." The man seems to the poet like someone met in a dream, "Or like a Man from some far region sent; To give me human strength and admonishment."

Admonishment, that is, for the poet's vain despondency, for his fears and lack of hope. At his request the old man repeats his story, adding that the leeches are scarcer than in former days, "Yet still I persevere, and find them where I may."

The concluding lines of the poem set forth the salutary effects of the old man's discourse:

> And soon with this he other matter blended,
> Chearfully uttered, with demeanour kind,
> But stately in the main; and, when he ended,
> I could have laughed myself to scorn, to find
> In that decrepit Man so firm a mind.
> 'God,' said I, 'be my help and stay secure;
> I'll think of the Leech-gatherer on the lonely moor.'

Faced with the bare necessity of survival, the leech-gatherer is a figure of fortitude and self-reliance. As much as the old man's arduous occupation, what strikes the poet is his natural dignity, his cheerful demeanor, and his simple eloquence, all of which put the poet's own fears to shame. Emerson, for his part, is critical of those who cannot live in the present but instead dwell on the past, or the man who, "heedless of the riches that surround him," attempts in vain to foresee the future. "He cannot be happy and strong until he lives with nature in the present, above time." To so live, for Emerson, is to live with God, and "when a man lives with God, his voice shall be as sweet as the murmur of the brook and the rustle of the corn." It is as if Emerson were thinking of Wordsworth's leech-gatherer, with his pleasing language and his courageous dedication to a humble task. For Wordsworth as well, the leech-gatherer is sent to give him resolution and independence. The 46th Psalm begins, "God is our refuge and our strength." Wordsworth echoes these words with his own prayer for God's "help and stay secure." Henceforth he will gain strength to find his way in life by thinking of the leech-gatherer on the lonely moor. The figure of resolution he will thus rely on is not one drawn from Scripture; the leech-gatherer, though exceptional, is a man of his own time and place. Wordsworth's inspiration comes not from above, but from around him, in the daily struggle of life he witnesses among fellow men and women.

Three years after the publication of "Self-Reliance," Emerson published an essay called "The Poet" in which he states his longing for the appearance of an American poet who would, with sufficient plainness and profoundness, address life as lived in "our own times and circumstance." Whitman that year, 1844, was still writing journalism for the New York papers. It was not until 1855 that he published *Leaves of Grass*, exactly the kind of book Emerson had called for, where the poet is "the man without impediment, who [...] sees and traverses the whole scale of experience, and is representative of man." Representative yet exceptional, in that the poet has the greatest power to receive experience and to impart its impressions in speech. Whitman also represents the virtues of self-reliance, both in his own practice and in the lives he celebrates. Where Emerson called for a new independence from classical models in art, Whitman puts that independence into practice. He is the first poet to write free verse in English, abandoning fixed rhyme and meter in favor of sounds and rhythms that arise organically, like leaves of grass: his long verse line and his extensive catalogues are designed to be commensurate with the immensity of the American landscape and the expansive movement of its people. Absent in Whitman are mythological allusions and traditional poetic models: it is all spontaneous song. There is nonetheless a richness of internal rhythm and rhyme in the pure lyricism of a line like the following, from "Crossing Brooklyn Ferry": "The sea-gulls oscillating their bodies, the hay-boat in the twilight, and the belated lighter."

An introductory poem in *Leaves of Grass* announces

> A book separate, not link'd with the rest nor felt by the intellect,
> But you ye latencies will thrill to every page.

Characteristically, Whitman directly addresses the "latencies" of poetic language, as if calling them forth into the light. Another poem invokes the memory of "dead poets, philosophs, priests, Martyrs, artists, inventors, governments long since, Language-shapers on other shores." Whitman freely acknowledges the greatness of what has been achieved in the past—"nothing can ever be greater," but then dismisses it: "I stand in my place with my own day here." A new world has come into being; a new wisdom and a new poetic speech are needed to do it justice. The centerpiece of Whitman's book is his "Song of Myself," which promises a new kind of experience to the reader:

> You shall no longer take things at second or third hand, nor look through the
>   eyes of the dead, nor feed on the spectres in books,
> You shall not look through my eyes either, nor take things from me,
> You shall listen to all sides and filter them from your self.

The reader is thus invited to be free of outside authority, even that of Whitman himself, in order to see and to judge life "your self." Another poem asks, "Have we not darken'd and dazed ourselves with books long enough?" Yet another assures us that the poet is sufficient unto himself: "I need no assurances, I am a man who is pre-occupied of his own soul": he has taken possession of his soul before others can do so.

Emerson found the origins of self-reliance in nature, and Whitman also finds it in the oak tree, the songbird, even the domestic animals of the farm. These lines are from "Song of Myself":

> I think I could turn and live with animals, they are so placid and self-contain'd,
> I stand and look at them long and long.
>
> They do not sweat and whine about their condition,
> They do not lie awake in the dark and weep for their sins,
> They do not make me sick discussing their duty to God,
> Not one is dissatisfied, not one is demented with the mania of owning things,

Not one kneels to another, nor to his kind that lived thousands of years ago,
Not one is respectable or unhappy over the whole earth.

So they show their relations to me and I accept them,
They bring me tokens of myself, they evince them plainly in their possession.

The animals' placidity and above all their self-containment are a powerful attraction to the poet: he looks at them with feelings of profound affinity. Their character is then defined in terms of the things they don't do that human beings do: whine about their condition, weep for their sins, discuss their duty to God. They are satisfied with life, they do not want to own things, they bow down neither to their ancestors nor to their fellow creatures. They care not for respectability. They are not unhappy, indeed the human idea of being happy or unhappy has nothing to do with them. They show all this to the poet, in the sense that in them all this is evident to him. He finds "tokens" of himself in them, in their self-containment.

Emerson's model of self-reliance, we recall, was social as well as natural and individual. He applies it to the world of work. If a young college graduate fails to obtain a professional position in a Boston or a New York firm, society considers him a failure. But for Emerson, "a sturdy lad from New Hampshire or Vermont who in turn […] *teams* it, *farms* it, *peddles*, keeps a school, preaches, edits a newspaper, goes to Congress, buys a township, and so forth […] is worth a hundred of these city dolls." Emerson adopts the vernacular language in order to convey the versatility of those self-reliant and enterprising individuals who, no matter what happens, will always fall on their feet. Whitman likewise celebrates the independent spirit of work in "A Song for Occupations." In this poem, he addresses directly the "workmen and workwomen" of his country and declares his solidarity with them. They are not to think the President greater than they, the rich better off, or the learned wiser. As for old institutions, libraries, and the arts, and religion, he tells his audience:

They have all grown out of you, and may grow out of you still,
It is not they who give the life, it is you who give the life.

The great accomplishments of civilization are the products of the working people who have made them possible. Here Whitman names a long list of occupations, each in the form of an active verb, to convey the energy each of them requires: for housebuilding alone, there is the work of "measuring, sawing the boards, Blacksmithing, glass-blowing, nail-making, coopering, tin-roofing, shingle-dressing." The catalogue names dozens of other occupations in this dynamic form: shipbuilding, coal mining, iron forging, stone cutting, butchering, ice-cutting, sailmaking, brewing, cotton picking, flour milling, and all manner of factory work: "None lead to greater than these lead to." The final section of the poem addresses working men and women as sufficient unto themselves to find what is best in life:

> Will you seek afar off? You surely come back at last,
> In things best known to you finding the best, or as good as the best,
> In folks nearest to you finding the sweetest, strongest, lovingest,
> Happiness, knowledge, not in another place but this place, not for another hour but this hour.

We recall Wordsworth's encounter with a remarkable figure of courage and self-reliance, a solitary old man barely earning his livelihood through hazardous and wearisome labor. Whitman's vision is also of labor, but he enlarges the idea of self-reliance to include an entire people working to make possible a self-sufficient society. The lessons of self-reliance thus pass from nature to the individual to an active and productive population. The poet celebrates this virtue, even if the lesson of self-reliance cannot be taught: "You shall listen to all sides and filter them from your self."

When *Leaves of Grass* first appeared in 1855, Whitman had paid for the printing and done much of the typesetting himself. His name did not appear in print, but instead the frontispiece showed a daguerreotype of the poet in relaxed posture, the right arm akimbo and the left hand in his pocket. It is an unusual portrait for a poet. He wears workingman's garb and looks straight at the viewer, the very picture of bodily freedom and spirited self-reliance. A copy of the book reached Emerson, who found out the author's name and wrote to him: "I find it the most extraordinary piece of wit and wisdom that America has yet contributed [...] I greet you at the beginning of a great career." The appeal for a new voice that Emerson had made in "The Poet" had been answered. Whitman wrote back to him: "Every day I go among the people of Manhattan Island, Brooklyn, and other cities, and among the young men, to discover the spirit of them, and to refresh myself." He reminds us that self-reliance is not solitude. The poet is independent in his work, but his inspiration is constantly refreshed by others, in whom he discovers the spirit he celebrates with such freedom.

Wordsworth's inspiration occurs in dialogue with a stranger, while Whitman's is grounded in democratic observation. But these of course are not the only forms of self-reliance available to the poet or to the reader, as a poet like Emily Dickinson demonstrates with a brilliance in which the pure distillation of her language is as much a departure from classical forms as is the unfettered expansiveness of Whitman's. Dickinson celebrates the absolute sovereignty of the soul:

> The Soul selects her own society—
> Then—shuts the door—
> To her divine majority—
> Present no more—
>
> Unmoved—she notes the Chariots—pausing—
> At her low Gate—

Unmoved—an Emperor be kneeling
Upon her Mat—

I've known her—from an ample nation—
Choose One—
Then—close the Valves of her attention—
Like Stone—

Dickinson wrote this poem in about 1862, a few years after the initial publication of Whitman's book. Though she claimed never to have read Whitman, the reference to an "ample nation" is curiously Whitmanesque. In any case, the sentiment of exclusivity is antithetically opposed to Whitman's all-embracing inclusiveness. However, if Dickinson's is a poem of self-reliance, it is not one of self-absorption. The very first line puts the soul in the company of "society," even if a rather selective one. By her divine majority is meant her pre-eminence, which makes the society she has chosen sufficient to shut the door. The line "Present no more" is in the imperative mode, equivalent to "introduce no more": the society she has is enough. The second stanza shows the soul unmoved by the sight of chariots or the homage paid her by an emperor. What is implied is independence rather than arrogance. Her gate, after all, is low, suggesting that her select society, even if not of high rank in the world, is granted easy access to her residence.

In the third stanza the poet intervenes in the first person, distinguishing between the speaker, who testifies to the nature of the soul, and the soul itself. This allows for a certain critical distance on the soul, not without a certain ambiguity: what is the precise relation between the poet and the soul, and what is her place in the soul's select society? The concluding lines cite an extreme case, in which from an ample nation the soul has chosen a single being, then closed its attention to the world entirely. We are left to wonder whether this being is the poet herself or, if she is already closely identified with the soul, another privileged being. Like the other callers, we are not admitted to the intimate sphere to which the poem refers. In any case the comparison of the "valves" of attention to "stone" heightens the tension at work in the poem: a valve is a mechanical device but also a natural organ, like the valves of the heart. For it to be likened to "stone," like that which sealed the tomb of Christ, puts the living soul into a tomb and so shuts it off from life, save that which is shared by the one chosen. The closing of the soul's attention is the closing of the poem, leaving the reader faced with a closed door of stone. Seemingly, no conclusion could be more emphatic, yet the ambivalence remains: is the poem a celebration of the soul's sovereignty or a warning against the temptations of excessive solitude? It is no doubt both, and may reflect Dickinson's ambivalence concerning both the solitary life she has chosen and the question of publishing her work.

Writing to Dickinson in 1869, Thomas Wentworth Higginson attempted to persuade her to meet him in Boston. Among the attractions of the city, he mentions a reading by Emerson and a meeting of a ladies' literary club. He adds, "It is hard to understand how you can live so alone, with thoughts of such a quality coming up in you. [...] Yet it isolates one anywhere to think beyond a certain point or have such luminous flashes as come to you." Dickinson did not accept the invitation. Earlier she had written to Higginson in response to his suggestions on publication: "I smile when you suggest that I delay 'to publish,' that [i.e. publication] being foreign to my thought as firmament to fin." She adds, "If fame belonged to me, I could not scape her." She seems to regard fame as both a trap and a profanation of her work. We know that of the handful of poems she published during her lifetime none carries her name, as if she wanted to send her "letter to the world" while escaping the perils of personal fame. In any case, her predominant attitude toward publication is expressed in the poem beginning "Publication—is the Auction Of the mind of Man," and ending with the imperative: "reduce no Human Spirit To Disgrace of Price."

Dickinson's writings on solitude and publication are those of an independent mind and imagination attempting to come to terms with the world around her. But wherever her inspiration comes from, her joy is felt within:

> Exhilaration—is within—
> There can no Outer Wine
> So royally intoxicate
> As that diviner Brand
>
> The Soul achieves—Herself—
> To drink—or set away
> For Visitor—Or Sacrament—
> 'Tis not of Holiday
>
> To stimulate a Man
> Who hath the Ample Rhine
> Within his Closet—Best you can
> Exhale in offering.

Exhilaration, with its prefix meaning "out of" or "forth," is the pouring forth of joy, in this case from an inner source. Dickinson draws on the metaphor of intoxication to convey what Wordsworth calls joy, intensifying for her the ecstasy of the feeling. This intoxication is generated by the soul alone, without need of other wine. In designating it the "diviner Brand," Dickinson initiates a play on the dual contexts in which wine is drunk, both at social gatherings and in the sacrament of the Holy Communion. The second stanza says that the soul succeeds by herself in the making and serving of the wine, choosing whether to drink it herself, to set it aside for a visitor, or for "sacrament." What would otherwise be a contrast between the profane and the sacred is made into a choice between equally worthy alternatives, given the exalted state of the poet's soul, which "achieves" the substance of the wine.

The final lines formulate a kind of maxim. The vulgar drink of holiday celebrations will not inspire the man with a well-stocked wine cellar, who has the "Ample Rhine" within his closet. The best to offer him is that which is "exhaled" from within. "Exhale," the first word of the last line, stands parallel to the poem's first word, "Exhilaration," forming an approximate equivalence between them. Dickinson employs an old use of "exhale," meaning to draw forth. In Shakespeare's day one could exhale a sword from its scabbard, and beautiful words could exhale tears of joy from those hearing them. Dickinson's exhilarating wine is thus drawn from her own depths and given as an "offering," again with the double meaning of what one offers a guest and the offering made during a religious service. The twelve brief lines of this poem thus achieve a kind of fermentation of its three main ingredients: the intoxication of wine, the miracle of the wine's transformation in the sacrament, and the deep joy to be found within the poet's soul. But once again, the poem resists the temptation of exclusive solitude. The allusions to communion and to drinking, the very idea of offering—these elements of the poem suggest that if exhilaration is within, it can also be "exhaled" and given to others to partake of it. The soul is not less strong, it is more powerful for doing so. Dickinson understands this; it is the reason why she has left us her poems.

The various notions of self-reliance found in Wordsworth, Whitman, and Dickinson share a sense that there is little else to rely on. If the poets of an earlier age could simply put their trust in God, those of the nineteenth century found it more difficult to do so, and so they sought solace in enlarged ideas of the human soul and human fellowship. Wordsworth's resolution and independence, Whitman's freedom from institutions, and Dickinson's exhilaration from within: all belong to a human world that increasingly relies upon itself and upon the self, rather than divine Providence, as sources of strength and inspiration. Nowhere is this conviction more straightforwardly expressed than in a poem that has taken on a life of its own in popular culture. During the 1870s, William Ernest Henley was hospitalized for 20 months with tuberculosis of the bone. The disease had cost him his left leg at the age of sixteen. It now threatened his other leg, which was saved by the use of new surgical techniques at Edinburgh Hospital. During his stay there, Henley wrote a series of surprisingly modern poems in free verse on the different stages of his treatment. These were printed in his first book of poems, in 1888, along with an untitled poem in more traditional four-stressed lines of alternating rhyme:

> Out of the night that covers me,
> > Black as the pit from pole to pole,
> I thank whatever gods may be
> > For my unconquerable soul.

> In the fell clutch of circumstance
>   I have not winced nor cried aloud.
> Under the bludgeonings of chance
>   My head is bloody, but unbowed.
>
> Beyond this place of wrath and tears
>   Looms but the Horror of the shade,
> And yet the menace of the years
>   Finds and shall find me unafraid.
>
> It matters not how strait the gate,
>   How charged with punishments the scroll,
> I am the master of my fate,
>   I am the captain of my soul.

Written in the face of death, the poem is characteristically Victorian in its manly declaration of fortitude and self-reliance. It has become something of a cliché of the English public school stiff upper lip, but when first published it was new in its formulations, if not in its sentiment.

The first stanza is a kind of prayer of thanksgiving, but with considerable doubt as to whom such a prayer might be addressed: "whatever gods may be." More substantial than these uncertain deities is "my unconquerable soul": if the body is vulnerable under the surgeon's knife, the soul is not. The second stanza states the poet's stoic defiance of suffering and misfortune, and the third his fearlessness of the death that looms "beyond this place of wrath and tears." The poem ends with a forceful statement of the poet's mastery over his own fate, all the more vehement for its being grounded in little else than the poet's own insistence. The poem might be read in contrast to one of Donne's Holy Sonnets which begins, "Death, be not proud," and goes on to affirm the poet's faith that death amounts to no more than a short sleep: that past, "we wake eternally, And Death shall be no more."

Henley's poem lacks Donne's faith, Wordsworth's harmony, Dickinson's intensity, Whitman's sympathy, and the genius of all these poets. It makes up for these absences, at least in part, through the sheer force of its rhetoric. The poem was soon famous. Untitled in its original publication, during the next decade it was reprinted in newspapers throughout the English-speaking world under various titles: "Myself," "Song of a Strong Soul," "My Soul," "Clear Grit," "Master of His Fate," "Captain of My Soul," "Urbs Fortitudinis," and "De Profundis." The titles alone reflect the degree to which the poem was adaptable to being read in different contexts. The first two listed here recall Whitman's "Song of Myself." "Clear Grit" alludes to Canadian political reformers of the time. "Urbs Fortitudinis" is from the Vulgate version of Isaiaih 26:1 and the "strong city" of the faithful. "De Profundis," later used by Oscar Wilde for his most confessional work, is borrowed from Psalm 130: "Out of the depths I have cried to thee, O Lord." In 1900 Sir Arthur Quiller-Couch, including Henley's poem in the *Oxford*

Book of English Verse, gave it the name "Invictus" (Unconquered). In Latin the word is used in different contexts. Cicero uses it for one invincible in combat, Livy for one who can stand up to the crowd, and Sallust designates "invictum Imperium" the imperishable Empire. Despite, or perhaps because of the changeable meaning of the word, it has stuck as the title of Henley's poem.

The multiple titles invented before the final one give evidence of the manner in which the poem has been appropriated by the public. After Quiller-Couch's *Oxford Book*, an even greater circulation was given the poem by its inclusion in Roy J. Cook's *One Hundred and One Famous Poems* alongside other popular poems of Victorian fortitude, including Rudyard Kipling's "If" and Thomas Babington Macaulay's "Horatius." Cook's anthology, first published in 1916, has gone through many reprintings. Over the years Henley's poem has been cited in innumerable novels, films, and pop songs. Nelson Mandela, during his 18-year imprisonment at Robben Island, used to recite Henley's poem to give courage to his fellow prisoners and himself. Something of the poem's indomitable spirit is echoed in Mandela's statement from the dock at his trial before the Pretoria Supreme Court in April 1964: "I have cherished the ideal of a democratic and free society in which all persons live together in harmony and with equal opportunities. [...] It is an ideal for which I am prepared to die." Clint Eastwood's Hollywood film of Mandela's life is titled *Invictus*, as are the games organized for wounded military veterans by England's Prince Harry. Henley was mentor to a number of young poets, including Yeats, who remembered the older poet as being like "a great actor with a bad part." He clarified this by saying that Henley was like "a great actor of passion" who displays "one quality of soul, personified again and again." That passion is for self-reliance.

Where Henley defiantly affirms the mastery of his soul, the American poet Marianne Moore engages in a quieter reflection on the nature of the soul given the human condition of mortality. Her poem "What Are Years" was published in 1941, as the title poem of a collection. The poet was 53. The subject of mortality may have seemed especially pressing given that her mother, with whom she lived in New York, was in her last years. When Moore herself died in 1972, Ezra Pound read this poem at the memorial service held for her in Venice. The poem originally had no question mark attached to its title. As Moore told her editor at the time, the poem is not a question; it is a meditation on the force of life, of feeling, and of human joy in the conditions of mortality. The poem's argument has nonetheless a fairly straightforward organization. The first part asks the question of how it is that human courage, even in misfortune and death, "stirs the soul to be strong." In the inescapable condition of human mortality, "All are naked, none is safe," regardless of innocence and guilt. Given this condition, what then is the source of courage? The poet remarks on the paradox that the soul is strengthened by its own defeat. The soul that "accedes to mortality," accepting its mortal condition, is compared to the natural motion of the sea. The sea rises from a chasm from which it does not escape, yet the chasm is the source of that surge; the sea even "in its surrendering finds its continuing." In like manner the living soul derives its strength from the struggle with its mortal condition. An immortal soul, knowing no threat to its existence, would have no need of courage.

The final part of the poem extends the metaphor to the image of a singing bird, who

> Though he is captive,
> his mighty singing
> says, satisfaction is a lowly
> thing, how pure a thing is joy.
> This is mortality,
> this is eternity.

Here Moore extends her reflection into territory familiar to Romantic poets like Keats and Shelley: the power of feeling, the figure of the singing bird, and the nature of joy. The one who strongly feels, says Moore, survives in the "struggle to be free." The very bird stands straighter as he sings, despite, or because of his captivity. And what the bird says is that mere satisfaction in life is not enough, that joy is a purer thing. "Hail to thee, blithe spirit!" says Shelley to the skylark, "Joyous and fresh, and clear," its music surpasses "all that ever was." Moore's bird is a kindred creature, and it illustrates the final paradox: "This is mortality, This is eternity." The struggle to be free is joyful; it makes eternity out of mortality. The contrast with Henley is not just one of tone and register; it is a difference in understanding the nature of the opposition between courage and fear, or more profoundly, between life and death. For Henley, the unconquerable soul is strong in the face of death, as a soldier is strong in resisting the enemy, as a sea captain is strong in the face of a storm. The opposition is absolute, between being and nothingness. For Moore, the courage of the soul has a more dynamic relation to death: it is death that gives us courage, and ultimately joy, by heightening and intensifying the sense of being alive. That is why the bird, though captive, sings, and why the poet does, too.

Taking Leave

The Book of Isaiah tells us that when Hezekiah was king of Judah, he was sick unto death. The prophet Isaiah came to him and said, "Thus saith the Lord, Set thine house in order, for thou shalt die, and not live" (Isaiah 38:1). The covenant of the ancient Hebrews made no assurances of salvation in an afterlife. Hezekiah was only 39; he believed that he had lived a good and pious life, and that he did not deserve to die. He prayed to God, and sorely wept. Hezekiah's prayer for a longer life was granted, but the story is remembered less for its conclusion than for the prophet's sense of urgency in exhorting the dying man to set his house in order. The story has a larger meaning, in that it poses the question of how to prepare for death. We are all going to die, but how are we to think about this? Is there a way to prepare to take leave of this world, to set our hearts and minds in order as well as our houses? There is perhaps no more important question in life, and it is one which poets have answered in instructive ways. Isaiah entreated the king to set his house in order; as poets contemplate death in their turn, they set their words and minds in order, in more lasting forms than the palace of a king.

One of the most famous of such poems is Shakespeare's sonnet No. 73. It is addressed to a younger lover who, in the poem's conceit, gazes upon the aging poet:

> That time of year thou mayst in me behold
> When yellow leaves, or none, or few do hang
> Upon those boughs which shake against the cold,
> Bare ruin'd choirs, where late the sweet birds sang.
> In me thou see'st the twilight of such day
> As after sunset fadeth in the west,
> Which by and by black night doth take away,
> Death's second self, that seals up all in rest.
> In me thou see'st the glowing of such fire
> That on the ashes of his youth doth lie,
> As the death-bed whereon it must expire,
> Consum'd with that which it was nourish'd by.
> This thou perceiv'st, which makes thy love more strong,
> To love that well which thou must leave ere long.

The date of this poem is not known, though at least one scholar puts it at or near 1609, the year the sonnets were first published. Shakespeare was 45, seven years before his death. What we do know is that the poem is written from the point of view of a man conscious of his age and of approaching death. In the first four lines, comprising the first sentence, the poet puts himself in the place of his lover, from whose point of view the poet's aging body is like the barren trees of late autumn. The poet's limbs, like those of the tree, may shake against the cold, and the vision of the trees as "ruin'd choirs, where late the sweet birds sang" remind us of the poet's vocation as a singer of words. The second quatrain, still insisting on the lover's point of view, shifts the metaphor of age to the image of fading day and setting sun. In the first direct allusion to death, nightfall is seen as "Death's second self, that seals up all in rest," tomblike. The metaphor of the third quatrain is slightly more complex. The poet's last stage of life is compared to the embers of a fire which lie upon the ashes as upon their own death-bed, a fire "Consum'd with that which it was nourished by." The ashes are those of the fuel that fed the fire, and which now consume its last remaining life—just as the life which nourished the poet's youth now consumes his body in old age. The final couplet returns to the lover's gaze, "This thou perceiv'st," this time with consequences for the lover's affection, for the sight of the aging poet "makes thy love more strong, To love that well which thou must leave ere long."

The sonnet's final couplet is ambiguous despite its seeming simplicity, and has been the subject of much debate. Is the poet making a simple observation, that his own aging makes his lover's love more strong? Or is he making a subtle appeal, as if to say, "You must love me all the more because I won't be here for long"? Both meanings are possible, and neither excludes the other. But there is a more interesting way of reading the couplet, one which touches more directly on the poet's own feeling. It is he, after all, and not the youthful lover, who is leaving this life. I tend to see the final couplet as a kind of projection in which the poet sees himself through the lover's eyes, and attributes to the lover his own increased intensity of feeling for that which *he* must leave ere long: not just his lover, but life as well: the sweet bird's song, the setting sun, the fire glowing in the hearth. Shakespeare's sonnet is a sly way of taking leave, in which both the poet's growing intensity of affection and his regret at leaving the world are deflected onto another person. But this is also, in its way, a demonstration of love, in that the poet is made to feel compassion for his lover's impending loss, rather than his own, which is much greater.

By adroitly turning the pain of leave-taking into an increase in love, Shakespeare's poem offers a form of solace. A generation after Shakespeare's death, Waller finds a more time-honored solace in the expectation that in leaving this life we enter into a new and greater one. The power of his poem lies less in this familiar assurance than in the lyricism of what has been called his "easy" style, where the rhyming couplet follows the natural rhythms of spoken English. Waller's "Of the Last Verses in the Book" is a leave-taking in verse. It is the last poem of the last book of his poems published in his lifetime, a year before his death in 1687 at the age of 81:

> When we for age could neither read nor write,
> The subject made us able to indite.
> The soul, with nobler resolutions deckt,

> The body stooping, does herself erect:
> No mortal parts are requisite to raise
> Her, that unbodied can her Maker praise.
>
> The seas are quiet, when the winds give o'er,
> So calm are we, when passions are no more:
> For then we know how vain it was to boast
> Of fleeting things, so certain to be lost.
> Clouds of affection from our younger eyes
> Conceal that emptiness, which age descries.
>
> The soul's dark cottage, batter'd and decay'd,
> Lets in new light through chinks that time has made;
> Stronger by weakness, wiser men become
> As they draw near to their eternal home:
> Leaving the old, both worlds at once they view,
> That stand upon the threshold of the new.

The poem is made of three stanzas, each composed of three rhyming couplets. The tone is one of entire tranquility at the end of life, where the soul looks forward to eternity. Despite the intensely personal feeling that inspires the poem, Waller's use of the plural "we" signifies the universal nature of his experience. In the initial couplet, the poet looks back on the loss of eyesight, in which the inability to read or write has been compensated by the power to indite, or to compose the poem: the failure of his eyes has at least the virtue of giving the poet his subject. The first couplet reminds us that these are not just the last verses of the book, they are "of the last verses," about the last verses. Waller suggests that they were composed without the aid of pen and ink under the poet's eye, but with the strength of the poet's soul. The loss of sight is thus made a gain, which the next lines extend to the more essential relation between body and soul: as the body stoops from age, the soul erects herself with nobler resolutions, not needing a body to praise its divine maker.

The first stanza having passed almost imperceptibly from the recent past to the present, the second puts the serenity of age in contrast to the turmoil of youth. In this way, the loss of youthful passion is welcomed as the advent of calm, as when a storm at sea, having spent itself, gives way to quieter waters. What is gained, however, is not just peace, but knowledge as well. In old age we see the vanity of youthful pride and the illusion of youthful affections: the emptiness of our attachment to "fleeting things." In the final stanza, the soul at the end of mortal life is given an even greater reward than peace and understanding. The emptiness of fleeting life is to be filled by an eternal fullness. In a strikingly original image, the soul's dwelling at the end of life is compared to a ruined cottage, where chinks in the walls allow new light to shine in. Ruin creates illumination. "Time" has made this light, in that it is the wisdom gained over time, given to "men"—to all human beings—as they draw near to their "eternal home." Waller here has shifted from the first to the third person, as if to avoid the vanity of claiming that wisdom for himself. In any case, the contrast between the humble cottage and the eternal home provides a further architectural metaphor for the poem's conclusion. Those made wise by time see both worlds at once, as they leave the old and stand on the "threshold" of the new. The consolation of Waller's poem lies in its compelling vision of a new life after this one. It arrives at that vision rather skillfully by means of a series of reflections designed progressively to gain the reader's consent: we can agree that poems are still composed when eyesight fails, that the soul gains strength as the body fails, that age brings calm, and a wiser understanding of the world than youth's vainglory. If all these things are true, and if Waller has led us this far, then why not grant the poem's final argument, that the wisdom acquired by time serves a purpose, allowing us to cross the threshold into a new world? It is, at the very least, a consummation devoutly to be wished.

Waller put this poem at the end of his *Poems written upon several occasions, and to several persons* of 1686. He followed it with a quotation from Virgil's *Eclogues*, a series of pastoral poems in one of which (No. 5) two shepherds mourn the death of Daphnis, himself a poet. Translated into English, the lines quoted by Waller say, "Bright Daphnis marvels at heaven's unfamiliar threshold, and sees the stars and clouds under his feet." How happy the vision of "sweet" Waller himself crossing that threshold! In his book, the lines from Virgil are followed by a single word: "Finis."

The position of Waller's poem at the end of his book, as well as its content, places it within the tradition of the *envoi*—the poem or verse which "sends" the work out into the world. Whitman's "So Long!" is another such *envoi* written, like Waller's poem, in anticipation of the poet's death. Whitman's poem is placed at the end of the 1860 edition of *Leaves of Grass*, as the final entry in a section called "Songs of Parting." Although only 41 when he published this edition, Whitman had a vivid sense that his life could come to a close at any moment. The opening poem of "Songs of Parting" is called "As the Time Draws Nigh," and includes the line, "Perhaps soon some day or night while I am singing my voice will suddenly cease." He then asks, "O book, O chants! Must all then amount to this?" But the poem ends in reassurance: "O soul, we have positively appear'd—that is enough."

"So Long!" then, concludes the songs of parting and the *Leaves of Grass*. Its title is a vernacular expression new to American English in 1860, and was not understood by many of Whitman's readers. In reply to a question from one of them, he wrote that it was a "salutation of departure, greatly used among sailors, sports, & prostitutes—the sense of it is *till we meet again*— conveying an inference that somewhere, somehow they will doubtless so meet—sooner or later." The use of the salutation is thus in keeping with

Whitman's desire to identify with the common people, and with his belief that no parting, including his own, is final. The poem has several movements, and goes from summing up the poet's work to a series of "announcements" for the nation, and finally to an intensely personal farewell to the reader. It begins, "To conclude. I announce what comes after me," thus rendering the conclusion of the book, and of the poet's life, the beginning of his legacy. He has dedicated his work to the nation, and believes that he has endowed its people with his own spirit of independence, freedom, and confidence in the future: "When America does what was promis'd, [...] Then to me and mine our due fruition." The series of announcements that follow are poetic decrees of national unity and joy:

> I announce a life that shall be copious, vehement, spiritual, bold,
> I announce an end that shall lightly and joyfully meet its translation.

However, it is the final five stanzas which most concern us here as an intimate farewell. Let us look at them in their full expression:

> My songs cease, I abandon them.
> From behind the screen where I hid I advance personally solely to you.
> Camerado, this is no book;
> Who touches this touches a man, [...]
> It is I you hold and who holds you,
> I spring from the pages into your arms—decease calls me forth.
> [...]
> Dear friend whoever you are take this kiss,
> I give it especially to you, do not forget me,
> I feel like one who has done work for the day to retire awhile,
> I receive now again of my many translations, from my avatars ascending, while others doubtless await me,
> An unknown sphere more real than I dream'd, more direct, darts awakening rays about me, *So long!*
> Remember my words, I may return again,
> I love you, I depart from materials,
> I am as one disembodied, triumphant, dead.

Whitman makes a significant shift in the poem by abandoning his "songs" and coming forward to address the reader directly as his "camerado"—a term of special closeness and affection for him. It is an extraordinary address in the way it is meant to transform the relation between reader and poet into a spiritual bond having a physical and sensual dimension. Whitman's book thus becomes his body, so that "Who touches this touches a man." The reader holds not just the book but the poet in his hands, and is in turn held there by the poet, called forth from his "decease" into the reader's arms. The reader's touch plunges him into a kind of ecstasy, "immerged from head to foot," until he has to call "enough" to what resembles an erotic union, a "deed impromptu and secret."

The poet's final "kiss," however, is not erotic but rather one of farewell from one who "has done work for the day to retire awhile." Here the poet leaves aside the figure of the book as his immortal body in order to imagine a kind of apotheosis, an elevation to a higher realm, with rays of light around him as he ascends to "an unknown sphere more real than I dream'd." His final words are of love, and he departs from this world "as one disembodied, triumphant, dead." This last word is also the final word of the book in the 1860 edition. The rest of the page is left blank except for an illustration: a butterfly alighting on the forefinger of a human hand. Is this the poet, transformed after death into a creature of the air, come back to touch us? His poem has much the same effect. It testifies to the real presence of the poet on the page we hold in hand, so that even in taking leave, he remains in contact with us. He is never really gone. As he says at the end of another poem, "I stop somewhere waiting for you."

Whitman's anticipated "translation" to an unknown sphere resembles Waller's step onto the threshold of a new world after death; both poets find consolation in the thought of another, greater existence. But Whitman's vision does not confine itself to Christian doctrine, nor does he see death as essentially different from life. As he says elsewhere, life is but "the leavings of many deaths." In contrast to the poets of an earlier age, and even to her contemporary Whitman, Emily Dickinson acknowledges a certain ignorance as to where we go after death. She thus looks back with nostalgia to a time when people *did* know:

> Those—dying then,
> Knew where they went—
> They went to God's Right Hand—
> That Hand is amputated now
> And God cannot be found—
> The abdication of Belief
> Makes the Behavior small—
> Better an ignis fatuus
> Than no illume at all—

In Waller's poem the soul praises her Maker at the approach of death, confident in entering her eternal home at His side. For Dickinson, who lives in an age of religious doubt, that Maker can no longer be found. Where we go when we die is a mystery. But this raises a problem for the living: if we have no faith, then what guides our actions in life? Is our behavior not likely to be small—petty, self-interested, materialistic? Dickinson concludes that it is better for one's way to be shown by an *ignis fatuus*—an illusory light—than to walk in utter darkness. This is less cynical than it may sound. Dickinson accepts the idea of faith as a guiding principle of life, even if the object of that faith remains elusive. But when could that object ever be located, or its nature ever known with certainty? Whatever her doubts, Dickinson's view finds at least some justification in the epistle to the Hebrews: "faith is the substance of things hoped for, the evidence of things not seen" (11:1).

Dickinson's thoughts on death take a more personal turn in a poem where her mortal condition is read as a death sentence:

> I read my sentence—steadily—
> Reviewed it with my eyes,
> To see that I made no mistake
> In its extremest clause—
> The Date, and manner, of the shame—
> And then the Pious Form
> That "God have mercy" on the Soul
> The Jury voted Him—
> I made my soul familiar—with her extremity—
> That at the last, it should not be a novel Agony—
> But she, and Death, acquainted—
> Meet tranquilly, as friends—
> Salute, and pass, without a Hint—
> And there, the Matter ends—

The poem tells the story of the poet's discovery of her mortal condition, as if the fact that she was to die came to her as a sudden realization. Her particular genius is to render that moment in the form of a death sentence delivered in a document which we read, as it were, over her shoulder. The reading of the document is thus a metaphor for her reflection on the transitory nature of life itself, and for the conclusion at which she arrives. That reading is steady and thorough, following the sentence down to its "extremest" clause, that defining the extremity or limits of her life. The sentence has all the forms of a legal document, including the date and manner of the "shame"—as if her death were execution for the crime of her own mortal existence. The pious "May God have mercy on your soul," is the formal closing, in court, of a sentence of capital punishment. The last six lines of the poem treat the poet's attempt to prepare her soul for death, in order that it not be caught by surprise. But she, the soul, and death, are already acquainted; they salute and pass each other even as friends: "And there, the Matter ends."

The seeming finality of this conclusion, and of the sentence itself, do not resolve certain questions raised by the poem. On one hand, one has to ask whether the death sentence applies only to the poet herself—her earthly existence—and not to her soul, which appears unmoved. In this case, the end of the "matter" would be limited to the poet's mere physical being, so that her soul, like Whitman's, might "depart from materials" upon death. On the other hand, the poet has made her soul familiar with her—the soul's—extremity, implying that the soul itself must come to an end. In this case, the soul's equanimity testifies to a deeply seated acceptance of death, as if her soul had prepared the poet to die rather than the reverse. This seems the better reading of the poem, as it enables the poet to rise above the crisis of the sentence and to share in the soul's tranquility.

As we have seen in Waller and Whitman, the moment of death is often imagined as the crossing of a threshold at the start of a journey. Such is the case in Tennyson's "Crossing the Bar," one of the best-known poems of the Victorian era. It is again a poem of farewell. Tennyson wrote it on the ferry crossing from the Isle of Wight to the English mainland in 1889, three years before his death. Like Waller's "On the Last Verses" and Whitman's "So Long!" it was intended as a last poem. It was published in late 1889 as the final piece in a collection of Tennyson's poems; before he died, he gave instructions that in all future editions it should also come last. The poem is written in simple alternating rhymes which develop the classical metaphor of life's ending as the beginning of a voyage out to sea:

> Sunset and evening star,
>   And one clear call for me!
> And may there be no moaning of the bar,
>   When I put out to sea,
>
> But such a tide as moving seems asleep,
>   Too full for sound and foam,
> When that which drew from out the boundless deep
>   Turns again home.
>
> Twilight and evening bell,
>   And after that the dark!
> And may there be no sadness of farewell,
>   When I embark;
>
> For tho' from out our bourne of Time and Place
>   The flood may bear me far,
> I hope to see my Pilot face to face
>   When I have crost the bar.

The poet puts out to sea at the end of day, when the sunset yields to the light of the evening star at the "clear call" of death. With characteristic Victorian fortitude, he forbids that his passing be mourned as he crosses the threshold of death, here represented by the bar of sand which protects the harbor from the open sea. The voyager of the poem ventures out at ebb tide, so that his vessel effortlessly follows the water's movement back to the "boundless deep" that is its home. The third stanza repeats the sense of the first in slightly altered terms. Sunset and evening star are replaced by twilight and evening bell, with the added image of darkness, as if to stress the poet's ignorance of what he will encounter in the uncharted realm toward which he embarks. The injunction against mourning is made again, this time forbidding "sadness of farewell."

The final stanza seeks to justify this stern interdiction. The poet explains that although the sea carries him out beyond our earthly limits of time and space, "I hope to see my Pilot face to face When I have crost the bar." These final lines project the poet into the unknown future, when, no longer "crossing" the bar, he has crossed it. In his humility he merely *hopes* to see his Pilot, without expressing quite the confidence of Paul in 1 Corinthians 13:12, who says of the kingdom of God: "For now we see through a glass, darkly; but then face to face." Is Tennyson's Pilot then the God of Christian revelation? Throughout his life Tennyson wavered between faith and doubt. In a memoir published after the poet's death, his friend Robert Bickersteth, the Bishop of Ripon, quoted Tennyson as saying that "we were not in a position to judge the full meaning of life; that we were in fact looking at the wrong side of things. We saw the work from the underside, and we could not judge of the pattern which was perhaps clear enough on the upper side." Tennyson added, "It is hard to believe in God, but it is harder not to believe in Him." In the end the orthodoxy of Tennyson's beliefs hardly matters for our understanding of his poem, one which for once can be taken at face value. In dying he will cross the bar into a dark and uncharted sea, where he hopes to meet his Pilot, that is, that Being who will guide him home. Among Paul's cardinal virtues of faith, hope, and love, for Tennyson the greatest of these is hope.

We have seen that old age and the approach of death can evoke different responses: an appeal to love, the anticipation of an afterlife, a calm acceptance of mortality, a voyage into the unknown. What we have not seen is a defiant resistance to death on the sole strength of human feeling. Such is the response of Dylan Thomas, a modern poet whose Romantic temperament would have suited the age of Lord Byron. Thomas wrote his most celebrated poem in 1947, while living in poverty and suffering from alcoholism. His father, David John Thomas, was a Welsh schoolmaster who, disappointed in his own literary ambitions, had taught his son a love of poetry. The poem was written as the poet witnessed his father's decline before his death in 1952 at age 76. It is called "Do Not Go Gentle into That Good Night." It is written as a villanelle, an intricate traditional form composed of tercets, or three-line stanzas in which the same two refrains occur in alternation: "Do not go gentle into that good night," and "Rage, rage against the dying of the light." Thomas's choice of this Renaissance form was made no doubt in homage to his father's love of verse.

The approach of death, itself the supreme imperative, incites imperative forms of speech. Tennyson sought to forbid the mourning of his passing; Thomas seeks to prevent his father's resignation to death. Insisting that "Old age should burn and rave at close of day," he urges his father to "rage" against the dying light. The demand seems peremptory, since the wise from Socrates to Tennyson have accepted their mortal end with stoic courage. But Thomas has another kind of courage in mind, that which consists in offering resistance to destiny, the very futility of that resistance being the measure of its nobility of character. Four successive verses give examples of different kinds of men who have, if not resisted death, at least fought it to the end.

Wise men know they must die, that "dark is right," but they have not given in to it willingly because "their words had forked no lightning"—they wanted another chance to make a difference with their words. Good men live in deeds, not words, and yet they too rage against the coming darkness because of the frailty of their deeds, never graced with the light and joy of fruition. They, too, are not ready to renounce what might have been. Wild men are those who have lived fully in each moment, who "caught and sang the sun in flight," not knowing the secret grief contained in passing joy. Their resistance to death is a desire to catch the sun again and sing a wiser song. Grave men see, in a final flash of insight, that their gravity has denied them joy, without making life longer or death easier. A little less grave, a little more blind, and they might have blazed like meteors, and been joyful. In the final lines, the poet turns to his father in a deeply personal appeal, uncertain whether his arguments will have effect.

> And you, my father, there on the sad height,
> Curse, bless, me now with your fierce tears, I pray.
> Do not go gentle into that good night.
> Rage, rage against the dying of the light.

Curse or blessing, either would be welcome from the father, either being a sign of the will to live. The two lines of the final couplet are those that have served respectively as refrains in the preceding five stanzas. The first urges refusal to submit. The second urges active resistance, however doomed it must be.

One reads this poem today knowing the fates of both father and son. David John Thomas lived for five years after the composition of the poem. A year after his father's death, Dylan Thomas died of pneumonia in 1952 at age 39. On the most personal level, we can see the poem as the passionate expression of the poet's desire to see his father live, and thus as an act of love. But the poem's excursions into the reasons why others have raged against approaching death permit us to consider it more generally as something like an ethical statement. This is one of those poems that have touched many persons not necessarily given to reading poetry. It has been set to music by Stravinsky and pop musicians alike. It is recited by Michael Caine in the 2014 science fiction film *Interstellar*. Part of its attraction lies no doubt in its celebration of a lost cause. Each of the cases of resistance to death cited in the poem represents its own kind of failure: wise men have not found the right words, the deeds of good men have failed, wild men have sung in ignorance, and grave men have missed their chance at joy. They all want another chance at life, which death will not grant. If we had to assign Dylan Thomas to one of the categories he describes, it would perhaps be that of the wild man, given his drinking, his affairs, his unsteady life, and his brilliant poetic voice. This is the poet who, in another famous poem, writes that "Time held me green and dying though I sang in my chains like the sea." He was one who, like so many poets, was destined to burn through life in a blaze and die young rather than to live to old age as his poetic powers declined. The call to rage against the dying of the light is thus as much a defense of Thomas's own life as it is an appeal to his father. Of course, life is the ultimate lost cause against death, and in this way the poem succeeds as an affirmation of life, a life made bolder and greater in its hopeless defiance.

I want to end this brief survey with a quieter poem by a lesser-known poet, John Hall Wheelock. Wheelock was for many years an editor at Charles Scribner's Sons, devoting his professional life to work often inferior to his own. As a twentieth-century poet, he is sometimes considered old-fashioned. He is called "The Last Romantic" by the editors of his oral autobiography, published 24 years after his death. One of his late poems, written in 1964 at the age of 78, is called "Earth, Take Me Back."

> I have been dying a long time
> In this cool valley-land, this green bowl ringed by hills—

In Romantic fashion, the poet places himself in a natural landscape, which becomes both the occasion and the reflection of his own meditations. The poem's title has prepared the ground for a peaceful tone in the form of a prayer to the earth to "take me back." We know from his other writings that Wheelock considered poetic inspiration to come from the feminine principle in human beings, and that the earth was the supreme embodiment of this principle. An early poem entitled "Earth" calls the heart of man the "earth articulate," and says that when weary with life we may entrust ourselves to her, and "lay Our faces in the common clay." In the later poem, the scene is one of reassuring enclosure, the hills ringed about like petals of a giant flower. The poet's place of dying is also a place of blossoming natural life in forests still wet from April rains. Night falls in springtime. Death is part of life, but is also an inexorable process, brought nearer to completion in the poem with each repetition of a few key words: "dying," "dark," "silent." The serenity of the poem is momentarily disturbed by the thought that when you are dying, "All things fall silent, or look the other way." There is a certain tension here between the poet's harmony with his surroundings and the loneliness of death. But this tension is resolved in the final lines, where the poet looks beyond the valley of his dying to the sky:

> There is a delicate haze over everything.
> Soft clouds are floating like water-lily pads
> On the dark pool of the sky. Between them,
> Stars come out ...

As if lying on his back, he sees the sky above as if it were below him, like a dark pool on the surface of which clouds float like lily pads, and stars come out from the depths. In this inverted perspective, the earth is the heaven to which he returns. There, "stars come out" as in the final line of Dante's *Divine Comedy*, where the Tuscan poet at the end of his journey has a vision of the universe made one by the love "that moves the sun and the other stars" (*Paradiso* 33:145). Wheelock's vision is secular and more earthly, but it apprehends a similar unity. His final line is suspended in an ellipsis as the dying voice trails off, as if restored to the earth from whence it came. Again one recalls Keats's nightingale ode, where the poet calls on death to "take into the air my quiet breath." In both poets death is "easeful," a gentle return to the mother's embrace, which redeems the pain of being born into the world.

Whether or not they endorse this view of dying, the various poems reviewed here have in common a vision of death that gives meaning to life. Shakespeare's sonnet is ultimately a poem of love; Waller praises the Maker of his existence; Whitman has endowed the nation with a new spirit; Dickinson lives tranquilly with death; Tennyson gives an example of courage; Thomas urges the living energy of rage; Wheelock affirms life's intimate relation to the forces of nature. In this way, each of these poems, implicitly or explicitly, has the quality of prayer. Some take the form of entreaty, such as Whitman's "do not forget me," and some are a more indirect expression of desire, such as Waller's vision of an eternal home. It is worth recalling that historically, what we call poetry began as prayer, as an invocation of the gods. Even the resolutely secular poetry of the present age has those qualities of prayer which consist in praise, confession, thanksgiving, appeal, or sanctification: the praise of goodness and beauty, the confession of personal weakness, the thanks given to life, the appeal to an ideal, the sanctification of privileged experience, or what Eliot calls "the moment in and out of time." When in the gospel of Luke one of Jesus's disciples says to him, "Lord, teach us to pray," (11:1) he is seeking words to imagine life and death in new ways. That is what poets do, and it is what poetry and prayer still have in common: the power of words to take us beyond ourselves, to enrich our lives, to speak to one another of our deepest fears and our greatest hopes, to humble, exalt, and console us.

www.ingramcontent.com/pod-product-compliance
Lightning Source LLC
Chambersburg PA
CBHW051615230426
43668CB00013B/2119